THE
CHILDREN
(Not the Adults!)
OF GOD

AUREANN,
May God Bless you
Each day As you live &
WALK AS HIS child
PASTOR JEFF TRUSE

THE CHILDREN
(Not the Adults!)
OF GOD

*"How great is the love the Father
has lavished on us, that we should
be called the children of God!"*

1 JOHN 3:1a

PASTOR JEFFREY H. PULSE

WINEPRESS WP PUBLISHING

Unless otherwise noted, all Scriptures are taken from the Holy Bible, New International Version, Copyright © 1973, 1978, 1984 by the International Bible Society. Used by permission of Zondervan Publishing House. The "NIV" and "New International Version" trademarks are registered in the United States Patent and Trademark Office by International Bible Society.

Scripture references marked KJV are taken from the King James Version of the Bible.

Scripture references marked NASB are taken from the New American Standard Bible, © 1960, 1963, 1968, 1971, 1972, 1973, 1975, 1977 by The Lockman Foundation. Used by permission.

Cover photo by Claus Bunz
Cover design: Ragont Design

ISBN 1-57921-446-0
Library of Congress Catalog Card Number: 2002100035

This book is dedicated to my wife and
children:
Sara, Nathaniel, Jonathan, and Mikal Soo

Wonderful gifts from God
and
great sermon illustrations!

Acknowledgments

I almost did not do it. I talked about it. Wrote parts, almost quit, finished writing, got disappointed, almost quit, tried again, got disappointed, and finally decided to really do it. It took much longer to go through all of these steps than you might imagine. It took a lot of help. There were many people who helped me—more than I can mention—more than even know. Some I will mention: My original editor, Betty Roed; readers and advisors, Daren Schadt, Marcella Harris, Rita Kubert and Carla Yenko; encourager, Sara Pulse (especially Sara Pulse!). Everyone of these people, plus many more played an important role in the development of this book, and I thank them!

I would also like to give special thanks for two wonderful congregations: St. John's Lutheran in Burt, Iowa and Peace Lutheran Church and School in Bremerton, Washington. I have truly been blessed by them.

Thank you to my three children: Nathaniel, Jonathan, and Mikal Soo. You will know why as you read the book!

Finally, thanks be to God in Christ Jesus!

Contents

Section Two: You Can Tell They're Getting Older

Have I Told You About My Kids Lately?

Introduction

What a blessing we have in our children. The Lord in His infinite wisdom has blessed families with children—children to love, children to nurture, children to raise in the knowledge and truth of God's Word. Why? Why would God entrust such precious and invaluable gifts to those who have a history of misusing and abusing other blessings? I really do not know the answer. Only the Lord knows and He has yet to reveal it. However, the fact remains, He has given us this blessing, these beautiful gifts, this huge responsibility.

I am the father of three amazing children, two boys and a girl. I say "amazing" because they never cease to amaze me, both in their value as a blessing and in the things they say and do. Now, I realize they are probably not at all unusual as far as children go (actually, I do not believe that for a second!). Many of you will probably think to yourselves, "My children did the same thing; my grandchildren do even more amazing things!" And I would never argue. In fact, you may be right, but these children that the Lord has given to my wife and me are a constant source of amazement.

As I write this introduction, Nathaniel David is six years old, Jonathan Christian is four, and Mikal Soo Roberta is almost three. My wife, Sara, and I often sit on the couch at night after the children are all watered and potted and safely tucked in and look at each other and smile. We smile because we recognize that we have been given something wonderful and rare, something that goes beyond the ability of words to express. However, there are those nights when we slump onto the couch and stare at the crack in the ceiling and wonder what ever happened to wonderful and rare! There are times when the words have to be held back, lest they say more than we really mean.

This is the nature of the blessing we have in children. They provide not only joy, but also frustration. They give not only moments of almost heavenly rapture but also severe, hair-pulling irritation. They give not only memories that can never be captured on film and video, but also days of worry and even despair. This is the kind of blessing children are, but still a blessing, amazing and wonderful!

After I say all of this, have you ever wondered why God calls us His children? If we were completely and totally honest with ourselves, we would not wonder, it would be obvious. Of course God calls us His children! This is how we act! We, the children of God, have the ability and opportunity to be a source of great joy and pride for our God, but so often we become a source of disappointment and heartache. The children of God resemble my children—your children—all children. How amazing to be made and called the children of God! How interesting to note that God never calls us His adults!

13

I am a pastor and my children become even more wonderful and amazing as they find their way into my sermons. As I struggle to find the right example, the perfect illustration, I frequently turn to my children. They seldom fail me. Sermons, Bible studies, devotions, they all become sprinkled with stories and examples provided by my children. I have also been guilty of using my wife as an example—a far more dangerous action—but my children are still young enough to be talked about on Sunday morning, without fear of later reprisal. So they creep into much of what I preach and teach.

I remind myself that other pastors do the same thing, perhaps with better observation and application and more justification. The truth that my children are no more amazing than any others is something with which I struggle. Nevertheless, the stories you read in this book, and the children who inspired them, are very important to me! The opportunity to share them is exciting, even more exciting than the opportunity to pull out the picture I carry with me at all times! By the way, have I told you about my kids lately?

But the angel said to her, "Do not be afraid, Mary, you have found favor with God. You will be with child and give birth to a son, and you are to give him the name Jesus. He will be great and will be called the Son of the Most High. The Lord God will give him the throne of his father David, and he will reign over the house of Jacob forever; his kingdom will never end." "How will this be," Mary asked the angel, "since I am a virgin?" The angel answered, "The Holy Spirit will come upon you, and the power of the Most High will overshadow you. So the holy one to be born will be called the Son of God." (Luke 1:30–35)

CHAPTER ONE

Where Does Jesus Fit In?

Gift buying for Christmas usually starts early at our house. Sometimes, even in the summer as we travel on our vacation. The chance to find that special something for that special someone—something unusual, or, even a little strange—often depends upon starting early.

One year, as we glanced through one of the specialty magazines, we found just the thing for Jonathan's godmother. Mary collects nativity scenes, crèches of all shapes and sizes. I do not know how many she has, but I know she received one more that year—a puzzle, a nativity puzzle— it was really quite the thing. If you took it apart, each piece could stand by itself and be arranged into a scene depicting the birth of Christ, or, if you chose, you could put the pieces of the puzzle together in its frame and it was still a beautiful, colorful nativity. It was the perfect gift for Mary!

I remember the day she opened it. She had come over to our home to exchange gifts the week before Christmas and everyone was excited. Mary is a pretty special person around our house, not to mention our hearts. She probably brought pizza—she usually does—but that is not what remains in my memory. I remember the grand opening! Everyone was watching, almost holding their breath, so excited about her long awaited reaction—Mary is a good reactor! She could unwrap a bag of rocks and make you think she had received the crown jewels. Of course, if the card said "From Jonathan," they would be the crown jewels to her.

Slowly the paper comes off—Mary knows how to make it last! She actually opens the card first (something I have never mastered) then she reads it, really reads it, contemplates the message, comments on the beauty of the picture—who can hold their breath that long? I am sure she does it just to drive everyone crazy. I know the children are almost beside themselves before the gift is revealed. Well, OK, so am I!

This time there is no question as to the appropriateness of the gift. This time the look on her face could never be manufactured. This time we got it right! You could tell by the wide eyes and the arched eyebrows, the little exclamation of joy that slipped out, the sudden jerk of surprise in her shoulders. This time we got it right!

It is a wonderful thing to give the perfect gift, and the children were delighted by the whole thing. They immediately showed Mary how it worked. They had been waiting a long time to get their hands on this present! They took it apart and began to put it back together so she would know how it was done. Maybe we should have let them play with it before we wrapped it up so Mary could have a turn. Jonathan gets the extra hug and somehow ends up with the best seat as they reconstruct the puzzle. One by one the pieces are fitted together until there is only one left, but something is not quite right. Jonathan holds the last piece in his hand, turning it over, a little confused. The last piece is the baby Jesus, but some other piece is fitted incorrectly, and there is no room. To this day I can hear his little two-year-old voice: "But, Mary, where does Jesus fit in?"

It caught me off guard. I just sat there as Mary fixed what was wrong and showed Jonathan where Jesus belonged, but I could not forget the question, "where does Jesus fit in?" Where do we place the Christ child in this world of ours? What place is given to the King of Kings and Lord of Lords? Good question, Jonathan. A very big question for a very little boy.

Perhaps the question had such force because it was the Christmas season. There is no doubt that Christ's place at Christmas has become confused. Many would not even miss this piece in their Christmas puzzle. For many, Christ is not a part, at least not an essential part, of the season named for Him. Christmas and its season, which begins sometime in September, is all about gifts—mostly getting. It is all about food—mostly eating. It is all about time off from work—mostly for sleeping in. And who can forget football and eggnog, decorating and light tours, family reunions and office parties? Maybe, if it can be fitted in, we will make our semi-annual pilgrimage to church. Something is not right! Some of the pieces are out of place. They must be, because there is no place, no room for Jesus!

How often are we caught up in this tide? Oh, we never leave Jesus out of our Christmas puzzle, but He is not always in the proper spot. Sometimes we have to twist and turn, bend and shove, to fit Him in at all. Too often He is the last piece placed.

The last piece, the leftover piece, the after thought, the last minute arrangement; is this the proper spot, the right order? Why not the first piece placed and the rest of the pieces around Him? Not only would Jesus always fit in, He would be the center of the puzzle of our lives. And why just Christmas? What about the rest of the year? Where does Christ fit into our lives each day on the calendar? The first piece placed and then all the other pieces seem to fit with ease. No forcing edges, or uneven, poor fits, every piece slides together with ease.

How easy to forget which piece goes where and which to place first. There is too much help that is not helpful. There is too much pressure to do it the world's way. Yet, the world has had a problem with order and direction from the day Adam and Eve hid in the Garden when they heard the Lord's voice. They no longer knew where He fit in, and they were even more confused as to where they fit in.

Maybe if we could know where we fit in with God we would be more likely to remember where He fits. It is no secret. God has told us over and over again just exactly where we fit in with Him. He has demonstrated how important we are to Him. Important enough to rescue us from sin and death. Important enough to redeem us with a sacrifice. Important enough that the sacrifice was His only Son. Why? This is a mystery, but I am sure it has something to do with His love. What is clear is that we occupy an important place with God.

This is who we are and where we belong. Our entire identity and place in life is centered around the love, grace, and mercy of our God.

So, where does Jesus fit in, Jonathan? Right in the middle, the centerpiece around which everything else has its meaning and existence. Where does Jesus fit in? He is the first piece in the puzzle. Then all the other pieces of the puzzle become a lot less puzzling.

The Lord is my light and my salvation—whom shall I fear? The Lord is the stronghold of my life—of whom shall I be afraid? (Ps. 27:1)

CHAPTER TWO

Whom Shall I Fear?

There she was, in all her glory, sitting on the piano, my daughter, Mikal Soo. Not on the piano bench, not on the keyboard, she was sitting on the top of the piano, grinning from ear to ear, clearing off all the knick-knacks her chubby little arms could reach. Just nine months old and could she climb! She had not yet mastered walking, but when it came to climbing, she was an expert. Stairs were a breeze—the furniture had all been conquered—she would climb anything.

When I came around the corner, I caught my breath as I saw her on her perch. I tried not to frighten her, even though my heart was pounding. If she fell . . . if she hit her head . . . if she was hurt . . . So, I smiled reassuringly and walked up to her slowly. No reason to worry about her being frightened, she felt safe and secure. This was her element. She was born to climb—God help us! As I drew near, I held out my hands to her, and she jumped right off the piano into my arms. I do not mean that she waited for me to take a hold of her before she jumped—she did not even wait for me to get all that close—she launched herself while I was still a couple of feet away! Yes, I caught her!

The boys were always timid about this sort of thing. They had to be coaxed to jump down one step as I held on to them—not Mikal Soo. I have had my heart stopped on numerous occasions as she has taken a flying leap off the top of the steps; just assuming I would be there to catch her. I was and I did, but what if I wasn't and didn't? Such a thought never crossed her mind. I am her daddy. I can be trusted. I have never let her down—never missed.

I am sure if one could read her mind, you would find a job description entitled "Daddy," and one of the main functions would be "catching." It probably comes right after "cuddling," "wiping," and "tickling." And, I am sure, somewhere in there she keeps track of successes and failures. And because I have never missed, I never will!

This level of trust is awesome—and frightening. Having someone look to you with complete confidence is a great responsibility, even a burden. Am I fit to carry such a burden? What about failure? What if I miss? What if I neglect my duty as daddy and she takes a fall? What would go through her head, how would she reason it out?

"Daddy can no longer be trusted. Daddy does not care if I fall down and get hurt. Daddy does not love Mikal Soo anymore." I could not bear it! I want her image of me to be one of perfection, and yet, I struggle under that load. Perhaps this is why daddies buy too many presents, allow too many freedoms, and forgive without discipline. We know we fall short, so we struggle to cover our shortfalls in other ways.

I did not get home in time to tuck them in and read a story, so, I buy a book. I missed the day she first dressed herself, so, I buy her new clothes. I was late for the recital, so, I let them stay up late at night and irritate the one who has to deal with them the next day. I know I cannot fill the shoes, so, I wrap my feet in all manner of fluff to increase their size and ease my burden. I absolutely do not deserve their level of trust.

Have you ever desired to be the trusting one rather than the one trusted? What a joy and relief it would be to have one upon whom we could place our absolute and complete trust. Rather than bear the burden, we could place the burden on someone else. But, there are no perfect people—no perfect daddies—in our world. We have heard and seen the flaws and imperfections. We have witnessed the failures and tarnished images. Still, it would be nice, it would be wonderful, a great relief, to have someone to lean upon without the shadows of doubt flitting before our eyes.

Well, there is someone—not of this world—but there is someone. There is a heavenly Father. There is One upon whom we can lean with absolute trust. There is One who has withstood every test, made every catch. There is One who never misses. His nature will not permit failure! Check out His record. When mankind made the fatal leap into sin, it was the Lord God who provided the rescue. The Lord made the move, made the catch, took the responsibility, even though it belonged to us.

If you are dumb enough to jump off the piano, you will just have to figure out how to catch yourself. The thought never entered my mind! *If you want to climb on furniture you had better be prepared to pay the price.* Never occurred to me. *You are the ones who disobeyed Me and ate the fruit. It is your problem, save yourselves!* Our Father in heaven did not entertain such a thought. He provided the rescue—but consider the cost.

The catch was made. Not with gold or silver, but with the holy, precious blood of His only begotten Son. God did not compromise His nature. He could have said, "We'll let it go this time. That's all right, next time you will know better." He could have said . . . well, actually, He could not have. To do so would be to go against His just nature. Sin had to be atoned for, payment made. God's justice demanded payment, but God's love and mercy provided the price. At great cost, at great sacrifice, He provided the Lamb for payment—the Lamb, Jesus Christ. The sacrifice was Jesus on the cross, painfully suffering the agony of hell, pouring out His lifeblood. And then the words, "It is finished," and God declared, "Paid in full!"

What a catch! The greatest catch ever made by a father. One-handed, snow-cone, almost-over-the-wall catch. God the Father continues His error-free streak. Each day we push it to the limit, look over the edge, take the risks, and the Father makes the catch. Each day He protects, provides, rescues us from danger. He has never missed, and, because He is our God, He never will. Earthly fathers dare not make such a promise, but God, our heavenly Father, can and does. His love and mercy are so deep and perfect that He never wants to miss. His power and strength are so awesome that He never does.

How wonderful! What a relief and comfort to have someone to lean upon without a shadow of doubt. He is always there. Each day as I struggle through my duties as father to my three children, each day as Mikal Soo tests my catching abilities, I hope and pray I never miss.

I know God never does!

Therefore the Lord himself will give you a sign: The virgin will be with child and will give birth to a son, and will call him Immanuel. (Isa. 7:14)

CHAPTER THREE

Waiting for the Baby

A dvent / Christmas 1992 is a time Sara and I will never forget. It is etched forever in our minds by the anticipation and excitement. We were waiting—waiting for a baby! Not the first or the second, the third baby; but this time was different. This time there was no due date. This time there was no swelling stomach. This time there was no kicking to see and feel. This time we were adopting!

Nathan and Jonathan came along in what is usually considered to be the normal way. They came with morning sickness, crankiness, doctor appointments, impossible due dates. They came in the way we had seen them come before as family and friends went through the age-old process—nine months and off to the hospital. When you come home the grocery list is longer. We had been through all of this twice before, and, even though no birth ever seems normal, we were used to the routine. This time was different.

Adoption is quite the process. We had reached out to the country of Korea for our third child. We filled out the stacks of paper, paid the fees, talked to the lawyer, dealt with Immigration and Naturalization Services. We had been fingerprinted, social-worked, and run through computers. We had been checked and approved by one adoption agency and two governments. We had been through the maze and now were waiting. Waiting for the baby!

Not so difficult at first; we were busy and preoccupied with the process. There was work to do and other children to concentrate on. We really did not dwell upon it, until they sent the picture! Our child in living color. Our child, newly born, on a one-by-one square of paper. Our child, half a world away, waiting for us as we waited for her. She even had a name—her Korean name—Soo Jin Jang. A name, a face, limited information, but no baby! Now we were waiting in earnest!

The picture came in October and immediately we called the adoption agency.

"How soon?"

"Between four and six months from birth, maybe more, maybe less, depends upon Korea."

"By Christmas?"

"Maybe, maybe not."

"How soon will you know?"

"Hard to say."

"When will we know?"

"We will call you seven to ten days before you need to be at the airport."

"When will that be?"

"Usually within six months, but you never can tell."

Obviously not! So we waited.

We moved into a bigger house. We picked over names. We argued and picked *a name*! Mikal Soo Roberta. Mostly, we just waited. Thanksgiving came and we waited. Advent went by and we waited. Christmas Day and still no baby.

Is this what it was like for the people of Israel as they waited for a Baby? They had a promise. They had a name. They had a place. They knew the circumstances surrounding the delivery. They were as close to having a snapshot as you could get in those days.

I began to understand a little better. I began to feel a strange sense of empathy for the faithful remnant as they waited. They waited through evil times and evil rulers. They waited through wars and rumors of wars. They waited through foreign occupations and exiles. They waited for hundreds, even thousands of years. They were waiting for *the Baby*!

Christmas Day was the easiest sermon I ever wrote, and one of the hardest I ever preached. I preached a sermon entitled "Waiting for the Baby." I announced to the congregation with joy that the wait had come to an end, the Savior had come. The world rejoices in this newborn King! I preached as I held back tears. Not tears of joy, not tears of thankfulness for the gift of the Christ Child, but tears of sadness, frustration, and disappointment—we were still waiting!

It was not that I was ungrateful for the Messiah. It was not that I had forgotten the joyful news of angels as they heralded lonely shepherds with heavenly anthems. I was joyful, I was grateful, I was excited, but the desire to be holding another baby . . . we continued to wait.

Then . . . then . . . the day came! The not yet became the almost! The day was almost here. We were almost sure when the plane would land. We were almost assured that January

15, 1993 would be the day. The waiting would be over! It was almost a reality.

I do not know how to describe it. The emotion, the explosion of joy, the relief, the excitement, the anticipation—the time was soon upon us! We packed the car and headed for the airport. The wait was almost over.

We stood at the airport watching each landing.

What time is it? Is this the one? Not yet. Running a little late.

The lobby was crowded, full of people, all waiting. Three families waiting for babies on the same flight. Nathan and Jonathan were losing patience with the whole thing. As they became restless and started to fuss, we found ourselves forced to think about them and their needs—the last place our minds wanted to be. We were focused on a plane, on a baby, on a little girl on a plane, soon to land.

Nathan and I saw it first. We had moved to the other side of the lobby, trying to readjust his attitude. We looked out the windows and saw the touchdown. We watched it taxi around the point of the terminal and saw it being flagged into the right gate. This was it! The long awaited moment had arrived.

I confess I heard no angel chorus, no bright star lit the heavens. I would not have noticed; my eyes were focused on the chute! Finally, here came the babies! Three babies— our baby—*the* baby!

Arm bracelets were checked and she was ours! The long awaited, much-prayed-for baby was here. As we held her in our arms, I thought to myself, *Had any other baby been so longed for, so impatiently waited for?* Well, at least one!

What a lesson a child has taught me. The joy we felt in the coming of our baby could not begin to touch the excitement of all creation as it leaped for joy at the coming of the precious Babe of Bethlehem. Having waited so long, having struggled so valiantly to remember, and, in remembering, to believe. Having recounted to generation after generation the covenant, lest the thread be dropped and lost. Then . . . *then*, the realization, this is it! This is the generation, this is the time, this is the place, this is the fulfillment. The realization that in the fullness of time the God of Abraham, Isaac, and Jacob sent His Son. The waiting for the Baby was over. God sent His Son.

The love of God came down. The love of God made man to dwell among us. The love of God, flooding light into the darkness. Sin, death, and darkness blinded, overpowered by the Light incarnate. A Baby that was more than a baby. A wait that was more than a struggle for one family. A Baby that was joy for a world. A wait that brought salvation and life to a cold, dead world. A lesson in love—God's love. God's love, which only God could deliver.

A lesson—but only the beginning of a lesson. Am I still filled with eager anticipation at the coming of the Lord? Does His imminent return hold me breathless? Is the excitement fresh and bold, or has it grown stale and old? The beginning of a lesson—a lesson in waiting. Waiting for the fulfillment; waiting for the culmination of the almost but not quite yet; waiting and having a faint glimmer of what the joy will be like. Too faint to completely understand, but enough to look forward to with unbridled anticipation and excitement.

A little child has taught me. Taught me about waiting. Showed me what fulfillment can be like. Taught me to understand that in the journey of faith, waiting is an intricate part. Our baby is home. The small wait is over—we still wait for that which is yet to come!

What I mean, brothers, is that time is short. From now on those who have wives should live as if they had none; those who mourn, as if they did not; those who are happy, as if they were not; those who buy something, as if it were not theirs to keep; those who use the things of the world, as if not engrossed in them. For this world in its present form is passing away. (1Cor. 7:29–31)

CHAPTER FOUR

The Old Is Passing Away

C hildren—children and the phases and stages they go through—what a fascinating study. Perhaps fascinating is the wrong word. Maddening, strange, weird, irritating—these words may be more accurate. Fascinating belongs to the childless. It belongs to those who have been there, never to return. It belongs to grandparents who take the small dose and then return the pill! These stages of childhood are best studied in retrospect when the desire to strangle has faded and only the "cuteness" remains.

As I write this, one of our children is going through a fascinating (maddening) phase. Jonathan is trying to drive his entire family to distraction. This is not something you would expect from Jonathan. Jonathan is the easygoing one of the bunch. He is the one with the deep dimples and the twinkle in his eye that will come in handy when trying to get a date or when he is in trouble. (Was that redundant?) He is the charmer. He can sit by himself all day and build towers, fire trucks, roads, or entire cities and only come to you for a drink of water and a little approval every two hours. Jonathan is the child everyone wants to take home with them, but they do not know about the "phase"!

Jonathan does not like new shoes. I know that does not sound so bad, but whenever we buy a new pair of shoes, he literally screams in rage and horror as we try to put them on. The fact that the old shoes are pinching and blistering his feet, the fact that he can barely walk because they are so small, makes no difference. Do not try to be logical with Jonathan about this; it will not work. Personally, I have found the best way to cope is to get up early and go to the café!

Unfortunately, shoes were only the beginning. I suppose if it were only shoes, we could adjust. There are many cultures in which going barefoot until age eighteen is perfectly acceptable. But, we go through the same routine with every article of clothing. New socks, new coats, new mittens, new shirts—a pattern?

At first, I thought it was an issue of comfort. Old clothes do feel better than new clothes. Just when I get my jeans broke in, my wife insists I not be seen in public in them. I thought it was all about comfort, but with Jonathan it goes much deeper.

He had a fit when he went from a regular car seat to the next step and again when he went to just wearing a seat belt. He had a fit when he went from a highchair to a booster seat and again when he began to sit on the chair. He had a fit when he went from a baby plate and baby silverware and a "sippy" cup to more grown up plates and utensils. Even today, when his younger sister is using these items, he will begin to look longingly to the past.

Jonathan's problem? He does not like change. He wants everything to remain exactly as it has been. He finds security and comfort in what he is familiar with, and his sense of adventure and excitement has not yet developed. What worries me is that this has been going on for some time, and I am beginning to wonder if it is not something permanent. Of course, I can always take consolation in the fact that he will make a good Lutheran!

Perhaps Jonathan is normal. After all, the fear of change is not uncommon and spans all the years of life, not just childhood. There is evidence of this everywhere. The main topic of conversation down at the café, right after farming, the weather, and the government, has to be "how things use to be."

"When I was a kid they never canceled school for anything."

"When I was young, we had to do chores and then walk five miles to school, and it was uphill, both ways!"

"Back in my day . . ."

"You think this is cold? Well, back in '34 . . ."

"Things sure were simpler when . . ."

There is a great attachment to the past and there is a great aversion to change. We like the old, the comfortable, the known, the stable, or even the instability of that with which we are familiar. We all have this within us. Deep inside we desire all things to remain the same forever.

Unrealistic and we know it! Change happens and will continue to happen. Change is inevitable—not painless—inevitable. Eventually, we will be dragged into the modern and new. Eventually, we must accept and even adopt change.

This is not to suggest that all change is good. History and personal experience has taught us better. However, history and personal experience has also taught us that some change viewed as bad or even evil twenty years ago turned out to be just the thing. But fear gets in the way. Fear of change, fear of the unknown, fear that grips like a vice in the face of the new. Fear goes beyond new clothes. It goes beyond computers and cell phones. It goes beyond VCRs and new math. Fear of change invades the fabric of our soul. It is even part of the Church!

In a religious climate that seems to initiate change for the sake of change, our orthodox antennae start to beep and buzz when we hear change for the Church being purposed. Rightly so! Change advocated out of boredom or the lack of anything better to do, or for the purpose of making a name for oneself, or to keep up with the religious "Jones" is neither proper nor productive. It does not serve the Lord's Church or His gospel plan.

However, change in the context of the Church is not evil. Consider the changes God Himself has wrought. When our world and its citizens were walking in darkness, God promised change. When we were lost and condemned people with no hope and no clue, God looked upon us and said, "This will not do! This must change!" When we struggled against the forces of sin and death, when we wrestled with Satan—and were losing—God in His love and mercy, said, "Enough is enough!" He changed things. The greatest change: He changed our world forever by sending His Son to live among us as one of us. He walked our walk, He talked our talk, ate our food, felt our hurt, suffered our anguish, and our world has never been the same. He changed it—He changed us!

The purpose of the cross was change. The suffering and dying brought about change. Resurrecting stamped the indelible mark of change upon the children of God. We have been changed from "not pitied" to the beloved children of God. We have been changed from "no people" to God's people. Quite a change!

God has changed us, but what does this mean for us as we live our lives in this world? God's change brings more change. Now we live changed lives. Lives dedicated to the Lord and His ways rather than the ways of the world, lives that revolve around God's Word, not our own selfish spheres, lives that look to the life to come, not the one left behind. Changed lives because we have first been changed by God's grace.

The Lord tells us that the old is passing away and the new is coming. There is another change to come. There is another earthshaking, world-transforming change to come. Christ is returning, and once again there will be change. Once again there will be a change that will bless and benefit His people. For those, like Jonathan, who panic at change, be reassured—this will be the last one! The final step of restoration, the culmination of God's plan, the climax of God's mercy and love. Christ comes again and He changes our bodies and our addresses. A glorified body—a heavenly mansion. Quite a change!

We live in this reality! This is a change we should never resist or ignore. As we look forward to this final and ultimate change, the word is *preparation*, the word is *anticipation*, the word is *watchfulness*. The old is passing away and the new is coming!

Jonathan will just have to adjust!

For God so loved the world that he gave his one and only Son, that whoever believes in him shall not perish but have eternal life. For God did not send his Son into the world to condemn the world, but to save the world through him. (John 3:16, 17)

CHAPTER FIVE

Lost and Found

The report comes in on the six o'clock news: Another child is missing! My gut tightens as I prepare for what comes next. A picture, the known facts, strange and suspicious characters seen in the vicinity, a police artist sketch—all of this flashed across the screen while a different pictures flashes in my mind. In my mind I see my children. It's their faces I see on the television. That's Nathan's age! Jonathan has an outfit like that! Mikal Soo is so trusting!

Only time will tell; only the ensuing hours will reveal the facts. Were they kidnapped or did they just wander into unfamiliar territory? Will someone be demanding a ransom or was it some "sicko" who . . . Will we see the parents on the screen overcome with relief or grief? Either way, my mind will once again turn to my children and I will vow to watch them more carefully.

What terror would fill my heart if my child fell victim to such an evil. What would I do? How would I deal with the loss? The hole in my life would never be filled. The void, the despair—bottomless. The loneliness, the guilt, the emptiness—a child is missing!

Where are my kids?

What would I do to bring the child back? What wouldn't I do? Anything—everything—I would stop at nothing. Which one of us would be different? There would be no price too great, no sacrifice too painful, no step too strange or bizarre. If there were a chance, any chance of it working, it would be tried. Anything to bring back a loved one, especially a child!

Where are those kids?

Then they walk through the door. They have been visiting a new friend they made at school. What's all the fuss about? They look puzzled. Why is everyone carrying on? What's all the attention for? Sure, you scold them, but your heart is not in it. The lost is found! Thankful, joyous, happy—the lost is found!

The lost is found, but when will you feel safe and secure again? The whole scenario makes me shudder. What could be worse for a parent? What could be more devastating than to lose a child to this evil and corrupt world? I cannot imagine!

For God so loved the world—a lost world, a missing world. Millions—billions—of souls crying out from the darkness. Billions of souls in danger of their very lives. Physical souls, but more tragic, spiritual souls. "Oh, that thou wouldest rend the heavens, that thou wouldest come down." KJV "Rescue us from this darkness, restore our souls!" And rend the heavens He did—for God so loved the world that He sent His Son.

Not that God was responsible for the darkness, not that He had driven man into his spiritual wilderness, not that the Lord had to restore and redeem. Man was missing from the presence of God, lost in the darkness of sin and death by his own fault. As a child who has run away only to find himself lost and longing for the home he has abandoned, man had run away in disobedience only to find himself lost in a vast and dangerous wilderness longing for God. So man sought to return. He tried to journey back, but the landmarks had changed. He found it impossible to return by the way he had left. He searched for another route, but every way was blocked. Every path was a dead end or a circle back to the same lost and condemned condition. Cold, lonely, afraid, he huddled in fear and bemoaned his fate and begged for mercy.

Those pitiful cries made their way through the darkness, through the wilderness, across the dividing chasm, and into the heart of God. He heard; rather, He felt, the anguish in those cries. He knew the torment; He knew the feeling of loss. He, too, was in anguish as He bemoaned the loss of His children. He knew the pain, the terror for His children as they journeyed in danger. He longed for them, for their safety, for a reunion with His little ones. He did what had to be done.

He was willing to pay any price. He was willing to endure any pain. He was willing to make any sacrifice. He loved His world, His children so much that He was willing to pay the price—He gave up His only Son. Was ever a greater price paid? Has a father ever paid such a ransom? What would motivate such a sacrifice? Boundless, inexplicable, immeasurable love.

The Father sent the Son. The Son suffered the anguish, bore the foreign sin, died to make the payment, shed His holy, pure blood. The darkness was pierced with light, holy and life-giving. The way was illumined. The path was cleared and the gates opened. The lost are ushered into the arms of their waiting Father.

They try to explain. They try to apologize, but He has already forgiven and forgotten. One thing matters—the reunion! One thing is remembered—the Only Begotten who went from heaven to Earth to bring the missing children back home.

Never again, we swear; never again, we promise. Never again will we stray; never again will we run away from the safety of the everlasting arms. But, the Father knows; He knows His children. He knows our weaknesses. He knows our good intentions. He knows. But He also knows that the blood of His Only Begotten will suffice to bring us back each time.

The lost are found. The children are home. The Father has stopped at nothing. He did what had to be done. He has gone the distance for His children—the distance between heaven and Earth.

For God so loved the world that He gave His only . . .

O Jerusalem, Jerusalem, you who kill the prophets and stone those sent to you, how often I have longed to gather your children together, as a hen gathers her chicks under her wings, but you were not willing! (Luke 13:34)

CHAPTER SIX

In His Arms

Children can be confusing! No great revelation if you are a parent, or a teacher, or a grandparent, well, maybe it is no great revelation to anyone! I have always had a hard time figuring out how children can one minute be running around laughing, playing, pleased with life, and then the next minute be clinging to my leg whining because someone they know perfectly well has said, "Hello! How are you?" I don't get it! What causes this strange transformation? How does this Dr. Jekyl and Mr. Hyde switch take place? Is this unusual? I don't know!

Nathan, our oldest, was notorious for this when he was young. The greatest challenge was story hour at the public library. We lived in a small town with a small library. The children all know the librarian. The children all know each other. The children all know the building. The children all know the routine. This was not a threatening situation! This should be a no-brainer for parents, right? Theoretically!

It was my day to take Nathan to story hour. As we walked, everything was fine, great! I wondered why Sara had that grin on her face when I volunteered to drop Nathan off. I thought to myself, "It's all in your approach. You have to have a positive attitude." I made a mental note to explain all of this to Sara when I returned home. Then we arrived at the library.

Suddenly, my son, who could hardly wait to get to story hour, would not walk through the door. He walked up to the door. He looked in through the opening of the door, and, suddenly, he transformed. Suddenly, Mr. Social Butterfly went into his cocoon. What happened? I tried psychology, I tried common sense, I tried reason—techniques that are highly overrated when it comes to dealing with children—I even tried bribery. Nothing doing! For a moment I even considered calling home to ask for advice but that would be a fate worse than death!

Finally, I told Nathan that I would go in with him. That worked! As long as I would be in there with him, things would be OK. Of course, I was the only parent in the room. And as long as I stayed there everything was fine, but when I tried to leave, he would transform! He would immediately start to cry and run back to my protective arms. So, I stayed, sitting on the floor, thinking about padding and chiropractors and other adult stuff.

Story hour lasted a lifetime. Finally, mercifully, it came to an end and we walked home. Nathan talked about how much fun story hour was the entire way. He talked about next week as I made plans to be busy. This is the Nathan who walked through the front door of our house. And there is Sara with the look, the grin. "How did it go?" she asks. I look her straight in the eye and say, "Just fine!"

There is something about a safe haven. There is something about having a place, a person, somewhere we can go and know we will find protection, love, and acceptance. Each of us needs such a place—each of us needs such a protector. We see this need in our children because they have not yet learned to hide it, but the need is there for each of us.

And Jesus says, "O Jerusalem, Jerusalem . . . how often I have longed to gather your children together as a hen gathers her chicks under her wings, but you were not willing!" Jesus promises refuge; Jesus promises protection; Jesus promises love and kindness and care; Jesus reaches out His arms to embrace the people of this world, but we are not willing.

So, we search the world over for peace; we climb mountains of intellectual achievement; we swim rivers of inner enlightenment and discovery; we sail seas of religious cults and sects, searching for sanctuary, a safe place.

How sad! What a shame! Jesus says, "Come to me, all you who are weary and burdened, and I will give you rest" (Matt. 11:28). And we still search abroad. Jesus says, ". . . how often I have longed to gather you into my arms. . . ." And we ignore His love. But Jesus does not give up. He knows our needs. He knows how much we yearn for what He has to offer.

Jesus is the One who has reached out His arms by coming into our world. Jesus is the One who used His arms to reach out and touch and heal and gather. Jesus is the One who stretched out His arms on the rough wood of the cross and allowed nails to be driven. Jesus is the One who held out His arms that the disciples might see the marks of the risen Lord. Jesus is the One.

And we still wander about. We still seek in unhealthy places. Then something happens. A tragedy, a fear, a disaster, a ruin, and we turn to run back to the arms of our Lord. Human wisdom and our law-soaked brains tell us it will be too late. There will be no one there. You left; you can never go back. You desert Jesus and He will desert you.

Wrong! In spite of our daily wanderings, Jesus is there, waiting for our return. Like the father waiting for his prodigal son, Jesus waits to embrace His wayward children. This is the love of Jesus for His children. This is the love that surpasses all human standards. This is the love that encompasses us regardless of unworthiness—the love of Jesus.

So, because we are the children of God, we revel in the warmth and safety of the arms of Jesus. We enjoy the feeling of sanctuary. But, as time goes by, we begin to feel brave. Like a child, we inch further and further away as we are tempted by our world. We step out further, wondering if we really do need the sanctuary, the loving arms. Maybe sanctuary is only a crutch for the weak. Then it happens— something does not go our way, a chink in the armor, the tumbling house of cards. Our world starts to fall down around us and we do not know which way to turn.

The world has betrayed us once again. We have trusted and been violated. What do we do? Where do we turn? We do not even know! But, there they are, the arms of Jesus! There He is with arms to bring us back into His presence, back into our sanctuary.

His arms—always there! Even though we are confused children at best, He is always there. Even though we continually struggle between saint and sinner, He is there. The loving arms never stop reaching, never stop gathering and holding. Jesus never abandons His children. We are safe in His arms!

But we had to celebrate and be glad, because this brother of yours was dead and is alive again; he was lost and is found. (Luke 15:32)

CHAPTER SEVEN

Fatherly Presence

Invariably, in this lifetime, whether we like it or not, we must eventually go shopping. As frightening as this is for some of us, the reality can be even more traumatizing—sometimes you even have to take your children!

In one such brush with reality, I found myself and two of my children walking through the front doors of a huge, self-contained store. Memory fails me as to the name, but it was huge! It boasted one-stop shopping and delivered absolute, total confusion. Aisle after aisle of things I had no idea existed. I stood there with my mouth open. Obviously, the thing to do was to get in, hunt/shop, and get out. I turned to my children and began to issue instructions: 1) *Stay with me!* 2) *Do not touch anything!* 3) *Stay with me!* And they did—at first.

At first it was difficult to walk without stepping on one of them, but then we passed that certain aisle. You know the one. The one with the toys! The one with the invisible magnet that works its wonder on children. One minute we are walking down the center aisle past the plastic, pre-scented, genuine artificial flowers, and the next minute I am alone! The children veered off, drawn by a powerful, irresistible force. I lost them! Well, not quite—I saw them leave. I saw where they went, and I decided this was a teachable moment.

I quickly walked around the corner and hid in the next aisle and I waited. I waited until they missed me. It took awhile, but eventually it dawned on them that they were alone, very alone. Suddenly, the store grew even bigger! Suddenly, they were confused and lost. Where did Dad go? They looked, but they did not find me—not at first. Of course, that was the plan, that was the lesson, and it was learned! At least it was learned for that day.

Sometimes, some days, as I walk through life, I am reminded of that shopping adventure. The world is a big place full of things I do not even want to know about. It can be a confusing place, a place in which to get lost. I know; I spend a lot of time as a pastor talking to people who are lost and searching. Some do not even know what it is they are searching for, but they know they lost it! Is this all there is? Is this all we can hope for?

Not according to God and His Word. According to God's Word, He created us to be with Him always. According to His Word, He made us to walk with Him, by His side, in His presence. He even told man: 1) *Stay with Me!* 2) *Do not touch that tree!* 3) *Stay with Me!* And man did—at first. At first he walked with God and enjoyed His company. But, the world is a very distracting place, full of glitter and excitement, toys of all makes and models. And, so, man veered off, pulled by the attraction to the things of the world. This was not according to God's plan, and it was not according to His plan to let man stay lost and wandering. First, however, He had to let man know just how lost and alone he was. First, He wanted man to be frightened by his separation from God. First, He wanted man to see the effects of sin and darkness. So God hid from man. Please understand; He did not abandon us, He hid His face from us.

Then, when the time was right, when the moment was full, when the teachable moment was finished, God sent His only Son to reunite us with Him. Jesus Christ is God come to Earth to rescue and redeem us from the sin and darkness. Jesus came to renew and restore our relationship with God and to remove the barrier between God and us. Once again, by and through Christ, we are in the loving presence of our Father.

We still ask the questions: "Where is God?" "Why don't I see Him in my life, in my world?" The answer lies in the more truthful and painful question: "Where are we?" The reason we have difficulties seeing the Father is that we are distracted by the things of our world. We have left His side and are touring the aisle filled with the things He warns us about. He has not left us; we have wandered from His side. Because of this ongoing reality, God has given us ongoing grace and forgiveness through His Son.

When I walked around the corner of that shopping aisle into the vision of my children, you could see the look of relief in their eyes. They never again left my side—at least not that day! Do they still wander? Yes. Do they still get themselves lost? Yes. Do I still seek them and take them back? Absolutely!

So also has our heavenly Father been toward us!

Even though I was once a blasphemer and a persecutor and a violent man, I was shown mercy because I acted in ignorance and unbelief. The grace of our Lord was poured out on me abundantly, along with the faith and love that are in Christ Jesus. (1 Tim. 1:13,14)

CHAPTER EIGHT

I Never Thought About It

I was a father for the second time. Another son, born March 24, just before midnight. Nathan, my first son, was two and one half years old, and he was excited about the possibilities a brother would bring to his world. It was the day after the birth and Nathan and I journeyed to the hospital to see Mom and new brother Jonathan. An hour's drive that lasted forever. Nathan talked and planned and questioned and drove me to distraction. How do you answer those embarrassing questions that little children come up with? I did what any experienced father does. I told him to ask his mother!

At last we arrived. We walked to the hospital room and there was Sara and the new baby. I got out the borrowed video camera and started the documentary. Nathan's fascination with his new brother lasted about three minutes. He could not get down on the floor and play so what good was he? Mom convinced him that in time it would all work out, so Nathan turned his attention elsewhere.

And there it was—something with buttons! Not clothing, but some mechanism that responded with the touch of a finger—the control for the hospital bed. He was on it like a fly on honey, and dear Mother made her first recognizable mistake, which could not be directly traced to me—she showed Nathan how to use it! If you push this button the back of the bed moves up; this button moves the front up and down. Nathan was in business!

At first, it was enough to push the button and see the bed respond, but soon it took more to satisfy his need for action. Soon he was seeing how far the bottom would go up. Then how far the front would move. Then how far the two would go together. It entertained both him and me, but there was one who was not amused in the least—Sara. You see, she was still lying on the bed!

All this movement would have been uncomfortable and irritating on any given day, but since she had given birth fourteen hours earlier, all the maneuvering resulted in some interesting expressions. It hurt! Nathan was too busy to notice.

Nathan did not want to hurt his mother. He did not devise this form of torture just for her. He was not out to punish his mother for having a baby who could barely drool, let alone handle blocks. He just never thought about it!

Me? I was rolling the film! I had figured out how to run the machine and I was not going to miss a second. Truthfully, I was so involved with the production that I never thought about it, either! Not to worry, Sara reminded both of us! She made us think about it!

How many times do we miss what's going on? How many times do we become so caught up in our own little worlds that we never think about the big picture? How many times does the trivial so engross us that the important is lost? We are so captivated by our own sphere that the whole world could collapse and we would not take note. Is this callousness? Selfishness? Apathy? Perhaps, but it is more likely that we just do not think about it. The big things escape our notice because other things, lesser things, have our attention.

This is also true in our relationship with God. So much of what we do is done without thought. We do not think about what we are doing or the effect it is having. We do not think about what our actions may do to others, or to us, or even to God and His plan. We just never think about it! Blissful ignorance. How frustrating this must be for our God who desires our attention.

As the created of God, our needs include the need to know what is going on. We need to understand that God wants our thoughts, our words, and deeds. The apostle Peter believed that Jesus was a great preacher and teacher, but he didn't think He knew beans about fishing. We, too, have reserved small pieces of our lives for God and His work and His teachings and His church, but we do not think this is practical for the nitty-gritty, nose-to-the-grindstone, daily life. Jesus said, ". . . let down the nets for a catch" (Luke 5:4). It was not long before Jesus had Peter's complete attention. He fell down on his face at the Lord's feet and said, "Depart from me; for I am a sinful man, O Lord" (Luke 5:8 KJV) . . . and not even half the fisherman you are!

Christ, the only Begotten of the Father, Christ, who is Alpha and Omega, this is He who came into our world. This is He who was humbly born and more humbly died. This is He who took ownership of our sin and took charge of the payment. He is the One who has changed our lives—not just a part, every part. Not just the Sunday stuff, not just the church relationships, not just the religious needs—all of our lives.

As with Peter, the Lord has sought our attention. He has shown who He really is and what He is like. More than a fisherman—the Fisher of Men. More than a shepherd—the Good Shepherd. More than a giver—the Ultimate Gift. The heavens parted and the Savior was delivered. Each day, as He walked the world, He sought the attention of mankind—miracles, compassion, humble servant-hood, a cross. How could we help but notice? How could we not rub our eyes in wonderment and astonishment? How could we ever again say, "I never thought about it?"

We believe, we confess, we teach, but do we think about it? Do we live it? Do we walk it—with joy? None of us has reached this goal of Christian faith. We are still sinners even though sainthood has been bestowed. We grant attention to the foolish and mundane. We divert to paths inconsistent with our faith. Do we understand? Where does this fit with Christ's plan? Do we think about it?

Then the Lord knocks: "Anybody home? Pay attention, I'm talking to you!" Usually not with words, but the Lord speaks; the Lord seeks—financial difficulty in the life of the financially astute, sickness in the life of the robust; crop failure in the life of the model farmer; family problems in the life of Ozzie and Harriet. Maybe a great catch of fish at the wrong time in the wrong place by a Carpenter. Maybe. It may be the wake up call we need. The Lord speaks; the Lord seeks. Why?

He knows that what we do not know can hurt us. He knows that what we do not think about can destroy us. He knows the dangers. God is a jealous God who wants our attention, but He is also a loving God who wants what is best for us. He desires our attention so we might receive the greatest good. He wants our focus because without it we risk our faith.

Not thinking, not listening, lack of attention can be negative to an eternal degree. So, the Lord knocks, the Lord reminds, the Lord calls. Not always pleasant, not always exciting, but always necessary, always loving. In love the Lord promised. In love He saved. In love He redeemed. In love He focuses and calls for our attention!

Have you ever thought about it?

In my anguish I cried to the Lord, and He answered by setting me free. The Lord is with me; I will not be afraid. What can man do to me? The Lord is with me; he is my helper. I will look in triumph on my enemies. It is better to take refuge in the Lord than to trust in man. (Ps. 118:5–8)

CHAPTER NINE

Let Me Help!

L ittle Nathan, our big helper! From the time he was able to toddle Nathan always wanted to help. Playing was OK, but helping was where it was at! For a time, nothing could be done around the house without that little hand tugging at my pant leg with the words, "Daddy, can I help?"

Just try saying no! I did a few times, but it was no use. Those pleading eyes, the hurt look, the sniffle—I always gave in.

I don't remember being like that when I was a child. Of course, I barely remember being a child. I would much rather have played, gotten dirty, been everything but helpful. Not Nathan! When we are outside and he is playing, all I have to do is walk into the garage and look like I am about to start some project, and there he is, pulling at my pant leg, "Can I help?"

It was a little distracting, but as he grew out of this stage, I began to miss it. Just when he became the age of really being able to help he stopped asking! Another mystery waiting to be unraveled.

Before this stage had passed, Nathan decided that his father was in need of help writing his sermons. I am not sure what it was that brought him to this opinion. I am not sure he was not right. I am not sure there were not others who shared his opinion. All I know is, one day after worship, Nathan walked into my office, sat down at the typewriter, and said, "Daddy, can I help write your sermon?"

At first I did not know how to respond. I have received other offers to help me with sermons. People are always saying, "Pastor, I wish you would preach about such and such and so and so." Once or twice, usually after using my wife as a sermon illustration, even she has made a few suggestions. But how could Nathan help? In the end, fatherly wisdom won the day. "I would love your help," I said. And I put a sheet of paper in the typewriter and set him loose.

Nathan was ecstatic! He knew what an important task writing a sermon was because he had heard me groan about the difficulties more than once. Now he was going to help. And away he typed!

At four years old, he was lacking in typing skills, not to mention being unable to read and write, but he made up for these shortcomings with determination. Five minutes later he was finished.

"Daddy, here is your sermon. What does it say?"

I took the paper out of the typewriter and read to myself: Wrobndgtan4rkgru8w,djnlmq.,m1O&iy4hj..kkks, kakjbax/';dd;;;;,hk/Kjjkdmsh kjyh,s kslyyt–40855983 pogujhgp,,,,,,,,,,,,,,hdiemdhnejk,fkqyd bgddgd&*%264) i74h—or something like that!

"Daddy, what does it say?"

Once again, fatherly wisdom kicked in and I read, "For God so loved the world that He gave His only begotten Son, that whosoever believeth in Him should not perish, but have everlasting life." Nathan beamed from ear to ear. It was just what he meant to say!

I would never say anything to Nathan of course, but how much help was he? He had all the right intentions. His heart was in the right place; his desire was to do the right thing, but the reality? He was unable to help. He was no help at all!

Do you feel a comparison coming? Consider the relationship we have with our God. The similarities are worth noting. We, too, want to help. We want to help God. We are constantly tugging, begging to help, but the reality? How much help are we? How much help can we be? How much help can the helpless give?

Think of the foolishness of the notion that we can help God. Unable to help ourselves we seek to help God! Lost and confused by the darkness of sin, groping around, looking for direction, seeking a destination. We are totally, completely helpless. So helpless that our wandering is not circular, it is a spiral—around and around, down and down.

Helpless, but we still seek to help God. We seek to help by giving directions. We seek to help by giving advice as to our condition and the proper steps required to overcome. We seek to help by taking charge of the details. The helpless seeking to help. A strange picture indeed!

Such is the depth of our confusion. So deep that heroic action is needed. Heroic action—into the darkness God sent His Son. Jesus Christ took action. He reached into the darkness and took hold of the helpless. He stood in our spot, hung in our place. He is the hero; we are the helpless. We could not bear; we could not pay; we could not! So Christ carried out a heroic action on our behalf and we are saved.

The helpless have been helped. We have been rescued from our helpless state and placed in a position to walk with God. We are also provided with a Comforter, a Helper to help us help. We can only walk this path with the help of the Holy Spirit. This is God's plan for us. His plan is to use us to help with kingdom building, but not our kingdoms—God's kingdom. This distinction causes us to falter. We have been rescued and now are given the opportunity to be helpful, but we still struggle to do it our own way!

We desire to build earthly kingdoms rather than the heavenly kingdom. We desire to follow our own scribbles rather than the blueprint of God. We desire to be the foreman rather than listen to the Master Builder. What is wrong with this picture? We have had to rely upon the mercy and grace of God to rescue us from our helplessness. We have been empty vessels filled by a gracious God and now we feel the need to rely upon ourselves to do God's work? Am I missing something? Are we missing something? Instead of using the new tools that God bestows upon His children, we want to go back and use the broken tools that belong to our dark past. We want to help, but we want to do it in our own way!

How much help? No help at all! Doing it our own way results in Jfgeinwkn kk73hfpjcj.,.q9.mmq;f/j/a/a/ [[[]ofja.kiya,gcfvwb.ncMjhsgfdkwqjjhjhgjhTRR&^%*ij 32u74yfw,,h,h,,o,lo,loh—or, something like that!

No help at all! So, here we are, broken tools wanting to help, cracked pots wanting to be filled, and at the same time, shouting out instructions as to how this will take place. It is enough to try the patience of a saint! How about God's patience? What a blessing that God is patient—patient beyond earthly measure. What a blessing that God still keeps us is His plan in spite of our desire to run the show. What a blessing! Through the Spirit, the tools are mended, the pots are patched, and the work of the kingdom continues. Through the Spirit, our wayward wanderings are redirected to the paths of God. Through the Spirit, our Negw,,wgkb;werlkwwu24 gwv9, ashfkiy3rl/..ep-.5u.o9yrlo\kitug. Hgfhvsshdf we,jurt272u2iuuglgldt. pt..s.jhvd;fww]ww[w['p-\wrw| becomes "For God so loved the world. . . . "

That helps!

But as for you, continue in what you have learned and have become convinced of, because you know those from whom you have learned it, and how from infancy you have known the holy Scriptures, which are able to make you wise for salvation through faith in Christ Jesus. (2 Tim. 3:14, 15)

CHAPTER TEN

Holy Habits

Bedtime! This can become the most beautiful word in a parent's day. *Bedtime.* Time for children to be tucked in; time for Mom and Dad to vegetate on the couch; time to wonder about a possible mix-up in the maternity ward. A beautiful word, a beautiful time—*bedtime.*

I have heard complaints from parents that their children's bedtime keeps getting later and later. I have a hard time understanding this. At the Pulse home, bedtime keeps getting earlier and earlier! It has everything to do with the sacred time of peace between the children's bedtime and the adult's. A peaceful, wonderful time to relax and contemplate, so we stretch it as much as possible.

Bedtime for the children takes on its own rituals. It begins with bath time. From there it progresses to tooth brushing, hair combing, and story reading. Then finally the prayers. We all gather together in the boys' room and say prayers. Jonathan and Nathan are in bed. Mikal Soo is on someone's lap and we pray: "Now I lay me down to sleep, I pray the Lord my soul to keep. If I should die before I wake, I pray the Lord my soul to take and this I ask for Jesus' sake. Amen. God bless Mommy and Daddy, Jonathan, Nathan, and Mikal Soo. God bless my grandmas and grandpas, my aunts and uncles, my cousins, and all my friends. Dear Jesus, thank you for this beautiful day. Thank you for all the wonderful things that happened. Help us to sleep good tonight and to have a good day tomorrow. And thank you, Jesus, for dying on the cross to take away my sins and for making me your little child. In Jesus' name we pray. Amen"

A beautiful, quiet, holy moment when everything comes together as a family—usually—sometimes—occasionally. Our desire, as parents, is that this would be the most wonderful time of the day, but there would appear to be another agenda at work in the minds of our children.

Just when we are ready to settle down for prayers, something blows the whole mood! Nathan decides that he is going to say his prayers in his head, not out loud. Jonathan refuses to come out from under the covers. Mikal Soo cannot make up her mind where to pray, so she jumps from one lap to another. Next thing you know, a stuffed animal wings its way across the room. Then the retaliation. Suddenly, our sacred moment resembles the playground at the local fast food joint!

Sara and I respond as do all good parents—we lose it! We try to take control. In order to accomplish this we use threats and force. After all, we have the best and most sophisticated weapons—we are bigger! And we win, usually. But the cost? Prayer time is now filled with sulking, sniffling, unhappy children, not to mention high-blood-pressured adults. It is now impossible to recapture the desired atmosphere.

A huge frustration! I want my children to love to pray. I want this love instilled in them so they will continue to pray throughout their lifetimes. On more than one occasion, however, I have thrown my hands up in disgust, shut off the light, and headed for the couch. Forget the prayers! They are not paying attention! It makes no difference to them one way or the other!

And what happens? It happens every time without exception. Every time I walk away without praying I hear about it. Not from God, not from Sara—from my children! The minute I sit down on the couch, frustrated, certain I have failed another "parent test," I hear my children.

"Daddy, we didn't say our prayers! We can't go to sleep until we pray."

And you know, they can't! If I do not go back in their rooms and say prayers with them, they will whimper and whine until I do. What does this mean?

There are three kinds of habits: Bad habits, good habits, and "holy habits." I believe my children have developed a "holy habit." They do not always pay attention. They do not always think about "why." They do not always appear to even care, but they have this habit.

I realize that there are positives and negatives to this holy-habit thing. If we do it only out of habit, is it being done for the right reason? Reasonable question. On the other hand, if we are not involved in some holy habits, will we ever develop holy patterns, like regular worship, daily prayer, devotions, regular Bible reading? Also a reasonable question. I suspect the answer lies somewhere between the two extremes, as it is in the habit of doing!

As a parent, I am grateful that my children are developing holy habits. What a blessing! Oh, that the rest of God's people would develop such habits! Oh, that my own prayer life was so regular that it was habit forming. Oh, that we would answer the distractions of this world with the words, "Not now, it is time for my prayers." "Sorry, can't make it. We have church." "No way! Can't go there. I have a confession." "Wait, I need to pray and study God's Word for an answer." Holy habits!

God's Word speaks favorably about holy habits. He seems very interested in you and me developing these holy habits. I admit, He is also concerned about doing holy things for unholy reasons, but He never mentions throwing out the holy habit because some would misuse it. It was God in the Old Testament who brought up the idea of passing along His commands to the children. He commanded the adults to talk about them when they sit at home or walk along the road or when they lie down or get up. Sounds habit forming! God is also the One who talks about tying them as symbols on your hands and binding them on your forehead; write them on the doorframes and on your gates. He wanted them to "bump into" their faith whenever and wherever they turned. He wanted a holy habit. God also talks about remembering the Sabbath day. He says, "Do this in remembrance of me" (Luke 22:19). God appears to be into repetition—pray without ceasing, teach them to observe, etc., etc.

All of this can be abused and misused, and, indeed, has been! But God never says, "Do these things until someone screws it up and does it for the wrong reason. When that happens, do something else!" Perhaps I am being presumptuous (not a small danger when dealing with God's will), but I believe God would have us correct the error rather than throw out the command. Holy habits, holy patterns were God's idea not ours. Doing the right thing for the right reason for a long time is part of God's plan.

Why? Did He have our best faith interests in mind when He inspired these words? Did He think we needed holy habits to keep us on holy paths? Did He see the bigger picture, the one we often miss? Of course! How do I know? God hit me over the head with an example—He gave me kids!

As he looked up, Jesus saw the rich putting their gifts into the temple treasury. He also saw a poor widow put in two very small coins. "I tell you the truth," he said, "this poor widow has put in more than all the others. All these people gave their gifts out of their wealth; but she out of her poverty put in all she had to live on." (Luke 21:1–4)

CHAPTER ELEVEN

It's All Yours

Feeding time at the Pulse "trough." Maybe a slight exaggeration, but those of you with small children know what I mean. There is nothing like dinnertime with three small children. Sara and I have considered drop cloths for dinner and shovels and power washers for cleanup. What a mess!

It wasn't so bad when we were in charge of the utensils. When we were doing the feeding, we had some control. True, there was the motorboat sputter and the sudden arm swing as the loaded spoon came in for a landing, but, all in all, it wasn't so bad when we controlled the silverware. Then came the rite of passage that forever changes mealtime. Then comes the day when, as a parent, you have to let go—of the spoon! What an exciting day for the child! What a traumatic day for the parents! Rite of passage or a disaster waiting to happen?

Each child handles this rite of passage in a different way. Some approach it with flair and creativity (none of ours did, but I've heard rumors). Others handle this freedom with all the style and grace of an albatross on takeoff. Nathan was not too bad; Jonathan was a wallower; Mikal Soo was—well, I'm not sure she had a category! Mikal Soo had very little desire to feed herself—she wanted to feed me!

Do you remember how difficult it was for your children to hit their own mouth? It really was quite a challenge for Mikal Soo to hit my mouth or for me to try to intercept the spoon before it was empty. As a pastor, I try to dress up and look respectable. I have never considered myself a fashion plate, but I have never wanted to resemble a dinner plate!

So, why did I go along with this? Joy! Not mine—hers! The joy she received from stuffing her dinner down my throat was amazing! Her eyes would light up, and she would giggle and laugh as she served spoonful after spoonful. Mealtime was exciting! She would get her bib, fold her hands, and grab her spoon. And she was not stingy. It was not "One for me, one for you." They were all for me. She had to be convinced that she also needed to eat. It was just too much fun to give it to Daddy. She had the true joy of giving—at least in the food department. Many times she would feed her entire meal to me and suddenly realize there was nothing left. It did not seem to bother her. She was trusting of her parents. They would not let her go hungry. She could give it all away and not have to worry about having nothing. She knew the providers, and they were generous!

And then there was this widow who had a mite, just a mite, nothing more. She gave it away! She gave it to her Father. She stuck it in the offering. How? Not, how did she do it? Rather, how was her attitude? How was the attitude of her heart? What was she thinking? How was she feeling?

71

"It's not enough to feed me anyway, might as well give it to God." "I bought all the groceries and paid all the bills, and all I have left is this mite. Let the church have it." "I'll give to God and His temple, but I had better see some returns or it will be the last time!"

Do any of these sound like the widow you've heard and read about? Me either. Why? No joy!

I doubt the widow was smiling and giggling as she dropped the mite into the box. Life and its experiences tend to suck that kind of reaction out of adults, but I am sure there was joy. A quiet joy. A peaceful joy. A joy from knowing grace. As Christ stood there watching—not watching people, watching hearts—He saw joy. She gave it all, with joy. She gave it all with the joy of knowing that no matter how much she gave she could never out give God. Her joy was founded in her faith. Her joy was strengthened by her trust and confidence. Her joy was strong even in the midst of want because she knew the Father would not withhold His bounty and blessing from her.

Such trust! "I am trusting Thee, Lord Jesus, trusting only Thee." Being able to have such trust must bring joy! The joy of a little child giving all her food, trusting that she would never go hungry. The quiet joy of giving all you have in the midst of crippling need, trusting, absolutely that the Lord will provide. Joy—how? Not so much how can I demonstrate this joy? Rather, how can I have such joy? Where does it come from? What does it feel like? Why don't I have it?

Trust brings joy. Trust is the motivating force behind giving. Trust is the fuel for our stewardship journey, and trust is based upon proof. Mikal Soo had never gone hungry. She trusted she never would. The widow had been provided for in the past. She trusted this would continue into the future. We have experienced love and blessings from our God in the past. We can trust this will outlast our journey on this earth.

Consider the proof. Man, deserving of nothing, receives the greatest gift. Man the ruination of creation receives restoration. Man the sinner receives the Sinless. Man the wanderer receives the Shepherd. Why? In the beginning, when things were perfect, when man walked with God, before the fall, you could understand why God would love us. Man was in His image and acted like it! A great time, but short! See how man reacted to such love. See how man treated such a creation. See how man dealt with being in the image. It was not enough. Man wanted more. He wanted to be like God. He wanted to be God! Man wanted it all! How could God be so foolish and love and care for us?

This is where we struggle and find the doubts that stand in the way of trust and extinguish joy. We see what we are; we know what we are. We know what we would do; we know how we would judge. No joy there! Not a trust builder!

Man's eyes verses God's eyes. We see ourselves one way, but God does not want to see us this way. God sent His Son to change the view. God sent His Son to wipe clean the sin that fogs and casts shadows. God sent His Son, not to rub in sin, but to wash it off. The blood of Jesus cleanses each spot and stain. The blood of Jesus changes what God sees. He now sees us through the blood and we are forgiven. He now sees us through the blood and we are clean and whole. He now sees us through the blood and He sees His children!

"I am trusting Thee, Lord Jesus, trusting only Thee." We can trust. We can be certain the Lord always blesses. We can have the joy! How? Because we have the proof. The proof is in the blood. The God who would not withhold His only Son will never fail to love, never fail to forgive, never fail to provide, never fail—never!

Joy!

Jesus looked at him and loved him. "One thing you lack," he said. "Go, sell everything you have and give to the poor, and you will have treasure in heaven. Then come, follow me." At this the man's face fell. He went away sad, because he had great wealth. (Mark 10:21, 22)

CHAPTER TWELVE

Mine, Mine, All Mine!

The sermon is finished and I stand at the altar and wait as the offering is received. My back is to the congregation and I am deep in thought. Have you ever wondered what the pastor is doing at this moment? What is he thinking? Is he giving thanks to God for helping him to remember and deliver the sermon? Is he contemplating the upcoming prayers? Is he worried about the amount of money going into the plate? Good questions, and reasonable guesses. However, while these things have crossed my mind as I wait for the ushers, I must confess that my mind often wanders. My mind journeys to faraway places and asks philosophical questions: "What time do the St. Louis Cardinals play and who is pitching?" "Did I remember to tell my wife about the potluck after church today?" "Was that couple in the fourth row sleeping or concentrating on the message?" "Did I turn off the coffee pot?"

I know this is a problem and I'm working on it! One day, in the midst of my meditation, I heard a voice. Not that kind of voice! This one was coming from the congregation. Not the whisper of God speaking to Elijah, not the firm voice from the bush speaking to Moses, not the voice asking for volunteers from Isaiah, it was a child's voice and it sounded unhappy. Worse than that, it sounded familiar!

Somewhere in the front pews my dear wife was attempting to teach the children a lesson in stewardship, and Jonathan was rewriting the lesson plan. Sara had given each of the boys a quarter to place in the collection plate. She was trying to teach them about giving an offering in church and the obvious approach seemed to be to let them do it. Unfortunately, in the short interval between receiving the quarter and the passing of the plate, Jonathan became mysteriously attached to his designated offering.

The plate came down the length of the pew. Sara held it in front of Nathan. In went the quarter as he stuck his head over the edge of the plate to see where it landed. She held the plate in front of Jonathan. He looked at the plate. He looked at his mother. His lip went out, his fingers closed tightly, and he proclaimed the quarter to be his! Nothing disastrous thus far, but there is a lesson to be taught!

Actually, there were two lessons—two lesson plans, two teachers—and the lessons could not occupy the same classroom peacefully. Sara's lesson was on stewardship, a noble theme. Jonathan's lesson was more earthbound—"Mine, mine, all mine!"

Sometimes retreat is a perfectly acceptable maneuver. Sometimes it is the wisest course. There is wisdom in living to fight another day. This is little used in parenting. Parents tend to subscribe to the idea of forging on ahead. There is a line somewhere that says something about fools being willing to tread places no one in their right mind would go. Must have been written about parents! Sara forged ahead!

She tried gentle persuasion, but, not having a lot of time to work with, she resorted to force. She pried opened the little fingers, extracted the sweaty quarter, placed it in the plate, and quickly passed it on. Done!

Not hardly!

It started slowly, softly. This was the whiny voice that first caught my attention. "I want my quarter back."

Sara whispers in his ear.

"I want my quarter back!"

Sara whispers again more urgently!

"I want my quarter back!"

I turn, receive the offering plates from the ushers, and quickly turn back to the altar, unwilling to witness the carnage.

"I want my quarter back!"

This is no longer a personal, child-rearing moment. The entire family of God in this place is now included. People are starting to fidget. Some are trying to hold back snickers—others should try harder! The cry of "I want my quarter back!" seemed to echo throughout the church. To this day I give thanks to God that Sara had another quarter in her purse.

Children! On the other hand, you have adults. We are much more reserved in these matters, but I wonder how often, as we drop the envelope into the plate, our hearts are crying out, maybe screaming, *I want my money back! It's mine, mine, all mine!* How often are we thinking: *I really could have used that money for the dentist bill. That would have come in handy when I go shopping this afternoon. I could afford a bigger car payment—a better car—if I had that cash.* It happens! We do not want to let it go.

As we laugh at children like Jonathan, we have the feeling we would like to join in on the chorus. Maybe the kid has a point! Maybe this is why we are called the children of God and not the adults!

Children! Children born into our world without resources, without trust funds, without clothes, without . . . They do not have the ability to provide for themselves. They do not have the ability to care for themselves. They do not have the ability to feed themselves. All they have comes from someone else. It is amazing how soon they begin to think that everything is theirs and *mine* enters into their vocabulary. Children! Children of God?

Is there a correlation? We are born into this world with nothing, or, more correctly, what we are born into our world with is worth nothing. It can even be dangerous. Our inheritance, our birthright, is sin. We are born with corruption. We are born in darkness because we are separated from God. We have nothing—nothing helpful, nothing worth mentioning—nothing that will remedy the problem.

The problem—sin and corruption—equal death and destruction. A problem of earthshaking, heartrending proportions. And, to make the problem worse, there is nothing we can do about it. We cannot overcome. We cannot solve. We cannot fix. We cannot rescue. We cannot restore. We cannot redeem. We cannot!

So we lift up our eyes from the slimy pit and cry out for rescue. We lift our eyes unto the hills and scream for help. Our help comes from the Lord who made heaven and Earth! There is help. There is a deliverer. There is a rescuer. There is Jesus. The ultimate problem solver for the ultimate problem. The lover of the most unlovable. The perfect sacrifice for the most imperfect. There is Jesus, and He fixes things!

Have you noticed the irony? God created the heavens and the earth and everything in them and gave it all to man.

Man messed up and God sent His Son to repair the mess. God takes the step. God provides the rescue. God bears the burden. God pays the price. God does it all—has it all, gives it all—and man cries out, "Mine, mine, all mine!"

All that we have is the Lord's, and we hang on to it as if we were the creator, owner, and deserver of all things. There seems to be some difficulty with role reversal. A steward is someone who takes care of something for someone else. When did God become the steward and we the owners?

"I will give the donation, God, but if You don't take good care of it, You will never see another dime!" "I stopped giving money to the church because I didn't like the new building project." "I'm not getting involved, nobody appreciates it anyway." "Why should I help them? They haven't lifted a finger to help themselves. After all, God helps those who help themselves."

These are adult versions of, "Mine, mine, all mine!" The title "Children of God" takes on a whole new meaning. Perhaps the word *childish* comes to mind.

And God did *not* say: "You can have My world to tend and nurture, but one mistake and I take it back!" "You prove to Me that you are capable of being good stewards and then we will talk about blessings!" "When you get your act together, then I will show you love, mercy, and grace."

God did *not* say any of this. Thank You, God! Thank You, God, for not being childish. Thank You, God, for being loving and generous. Thank You, God, for not withholding anything from us—not even Your Son. And, thank You, God, for our children so we can have a better picture of ourselves.

Endure hardship as discipline; God is treating you as sons. For what son is not disciplined by his father? If you are not disciplined (and everyone undergoes discipline), then you are illegitimate children and not true sons. Moreover, we have all had human fathers who disciplined us and we respected them for it. How much more should we submit to the Father of our spirits and live! Our fathers disciplined us for a little while as they thought best; but God disciplines us for our good, that we may share in his holiness. No discipline seems pleasant at the time, but painful. Later on, however, it produces a harvest of righteousness and peace for those who have been trained by it. (Heb. 12:7–11)

CHAPTER THIRTEEN

But I Still Love You!

Have I mentioned how much I love my family and how thankful I am for them? Have I told you about my kids lately? At this point, you may very well be tired of hearing about my kids! Believe me, I am just getting started! I love to talk about my family, especially my children. However, I have to watch myself, because I have the potential—often realized—of driving people to distraction with all of my "wonderful family" talk. People can only take so much of this. Unless, of course, you are talking about their family—that's different!

When visitors come by my house and the kids are asleep, my greatest desire is to take them to their rooms, open the door, and let the hall light fall gently upon their faces as they sleep. "Take a look," I want to say. "Aren't they beautiful?"

"Yeah, I guess."

"No, really! Look closely. Have you ever seen anything so precious and wonderful?"

"Sure, I suppose."

"Come on! Are these not the most beautiful children you have ever seen!"

About this time our visitors would be looking at their watches, feeling the sudden need to get home. Big day tomorrow! About this time I would be exasperated at their lack of intelligence in regards to my children. About this time I would have crossed the boundary. What I want to tell these people, what I want to tell everyone is "These are beautiful and wonderful children and they are mine! And, if you do not understand this, you are not the person of discernment and wisdom I thought you were!"

What causes a normal, semi-rational human being to act this way? Love! I love them deeply! I love them and want everyone to know that I love them. I want everyone to love them the way I do.

But here is an interesting twist: Sometimes my children question my love for them. Even with beautiful and wonderful children such as mine, there are times when I need to exercise discipline. Even these "perfect" children act in imperfect and unacceptable ways; therefore, steps need to be taken. But when steps are taken questions are asked. Sometimes the steps cause my children to wonder and ponder my love for them. *Does Daddy still love me?*

What's the answer? Of course I still love them—with all my heart! I never understood the phrase, "This is going to hurt me a lot more than it is going to hurt you," until I became a father and felt my heart ache as I disciplined. How do you explain that to your children? How do you make them understand that *because* you love them you discipline? How do you tell them that it is for their own good that you discipline?

This is a picture of God's love for us. An imperfect picture, because even a father's love for his children cannot compare to the Father's love for us. Still, a picture. Love so deep, so committed, so compassionate that it is not afraid to discipline. Discipline—love? Love—discipline?

How do you feel when the Lord hands out discipline? What are your thoughts? *Why me, Lord? What are You doing? Do You know what You are doing? How can I handle this? Who is responsible? Do You still love me?*

We have all been there. We have all asked the questions. We have all wondered. Why? It is important for us to know! It is important for us to know what God thinks about us—if He thinks about us. It is important to know if God still loves us. The answer may seem obvious right now, but when we are in the midst of discipline, our spiritual insecurity takes over!

"Father in heaven, do You still love me?"

God has an answer, but, as is often the case, we struggle to hear it because of sin-impaired ears. So God speaks in actions. From the times of old, He has spoken through His prophets, but also through His plan, as it took shape right before His people. A rainbow, a flaming pot, a burning bush, a strange buffet (all you can eat, but no doggie bags), a crumpled city, a beautiful temple, an altar on fire, a reconstructed temple, a voice of one crying in the wilderness. Right before their eyes God said, "I still love you!"

And, in these last days, He has spoken to us through His Son. Physical evidence, a visible sign of God's love. "I still love you!" Too often, we concentrate on the flat wallet, the pinched belly, the weak body, the pained heart, and we miss the message. "I still love you!"

A Son, an only Son, given in the flesh to be a payment. Not symbolic, in the flesh! Flesh can bleed; flesh can suffer; flesh can be wounded; flesh can die! In the flesh Christ came, and in the flesh He paid our price. In the flesh He rescued and redeemed. In the flesh He conquered. In the flesh He rose victorious. In the flesh he ascended. In the flesh He continues to come to us. Look and see, reach out and touch, witness and grab hold. "I still love you!"

The father who loves his children, disciplines. Not because he wants his children in pain; rather, because he knows a little pain today can detour massive agony tomorrow. The Father in heaven loves us with a love so far beyond comprehension that a comparison can never be adequate. His discipline today prepares us for an eternal dwelling. Observe the signs; see the proof. He still loves us!

so Christ was sacrificed once to take away the sins of many people; and he will appear a second time, not to bear sin, but to bring salvation to those who are waiting for him. (Heb. 9:28)

CHAPTER FOURTEEN

Not Yet Daddy!

Toys, toys, toys! When Nathan was born, Sara and I decided we would not bury our child in toys. We decided this was a terrible waste of resources, it sent all the wrong messages. We decided we would concentrate on higher things—college, imagination, educational stuff! We decided—but, as young parents, we neglected to inform the other interested parties (as if that would have made any difference).

We forgot about grandparents, great grandparents and godparents, uncles and aunts, great uncles and great aunts; we forgot about a lot of interested parties! We were too green to factor in being a young pastor and pastor's wife in their first parish, having their first child. Who knew? Who was prepared for that kind of attention and excitement? And the presents and the toys—they just kept coming!

One toy box was not enough. Two toy boxes overflowed. Finally, we broke down and purchased a big toy box and even that proved to be inadequate. The big toy box was always overly full, and, as you know, with lots of toys comes lots of mess! And, as you also know, toys never take themselves out of the toy box and they also never put themselves back!

On those days when Nathan and Jonathan decided to play upstairs in their room, we always wound up fighting the clean-up battle. On those days, the boys would take every toy out of the box and spread them across the floor of the room and out into the hallway. There is nothing wrong with this, technically. Toys are made to be played with and how can you play with them if they are still in the toy box? Besides, we never had the foresight to put a lock on that box! The problem developed when we discovered this was a child's idea of interior decorating. Toys on the floor, toys in the hall, toys in the way—a child's dream, a parent's nightmare! The battle begins!

Sara and I would go upstairs and tell them it was time to clean up. Put the toys back into the box, straighten the rug, scrub the floor, dust the furniture (its worth a try!). Then we would leave, but, as we walked out the door, I would turn to deliver the ultimatum: "When I come back this room had better be clean!"

Down the steps we go and leave them to their cleaning. And what happens? They start strong, but then they come across a toy that begs for attention. They begin with good intentions. They heard the voice of authority, they understand the instructions, but no one was standing over them to remind, and there were all these toys, and, well, you know how it is with toys!

We stand at the bottom of the steps and listen. You can hear it. First, the flurry of activity. Then the slow, tapering off. The gradual evolution from clean up to playing noise. At this point I yell up the stairs, "Are you ready?"

"Not yet, Daddy! Don't come up yet!"

We wait. We give them more time. More time to clean and prepare for inspection. The process is instructive: The quick start, the gradual fade, the giving in. Children!

"How are you doing? Are you ready? Is everything picked up?"

"Not yet, Daddy! Just a little more time! Give us a little more time!"

We wait. Scare tactics are in order. I stomp up the first few steps—what a reaction! The level of activity escalates— more like an explosion! "Not yet, Daddy! Not yet!"

The battle goes on a little longer, but, eventually, the boys are ready for inspection. Generally, they even pass, but only because of the nearsighted tendencies of loving parents.

I cannot help but visualize God in heaven looking upon our world in its disarray, in its chaotic condition, shaking His head and saying, "A little more time! I will give them a little more time."

I wonder if the disasters and other signs of the times are God's way of calling up the steps, "Are you ready yet?" And we frantically respond, "Not yet! Give us a little more time!"

On the one hand, we wait patiently, excitedly for the Lord to come, to bring fulfillment. On the other hand, we keep asking for more time. More time for preparation. More time for clean up. More time for garbage removal—spiritual trash takeout. All this time we have been walking around messes, but the long-awaited guest is coming. We want things to look good, don't we?

Jesus Christ came into our mess once before. He carried the garbage of our sin to the cross. He changed us from corrupted, disgusting, miserable sinners into the children of God, the restored, cleansed, redeemed children of God.

And, as He ascended into heaven, He promised He would come again. He encouraged us to be ready, to make ready. Do His work; prepare the world.

Have we?

The other day at the bank I was waiting in line. One thing about waiting in line, you are never alone! Unfortunately, you seldom have a choice as to whom you are waiting with! As I stood in line waiting, the woman ahead of me was beside herself. She had waited too long. She fidgeted, cranking her head from one side to the other, searching for more tellers to get the show on the road. She almost demanded the loan officer become a teller. Any warm body connected to the bank would do. (I wonder what would have happened if the janitor had walked by?)

The woman was all over the place, and I was given the responsibility of holding her place in line. I did not mind; after all, it got her away from me! Finally, her turn came. She grumbled and complained all the way to the counter, and, lo and behold, she was not ready! She had neglected to fill out a deposit slip. She had not endorsed her check. She was not even sure how she wanted to direct her funds. The teller would have made Saint Teresa proud; my thoughts would have made her blush! All that time to make preparation wasted!

"Come on, Lord! We are waiting! Come on! What? Tomorrow? It can't be tomorrow. My appointment book is full! Not tomorrow. Did I say I wanted you to come right away? I did not mean 'right away!' More like the near future. You know, after the kids graduate, or something like that. . . ."

Just a little more time! Thus far we have been given a little more time. A few more moments to spread the Word. A few more moments to talk to our neighbor. A few more moments to visit with a relative. A few more moments to send a missionary to China. A few more moments to build the outreach at church. A few more moments, a little more time. . . .

How much longer? We worry about how long and fail to take advantage of the time. We ask, "How long?" But isn't "How much more?" the better question? How much more work to do? How many more people to reach? How many more Bibles to deliver? How many more souls to enlighten? How much more harvesting of the heavenly crop?

Come, Lord Jesus, quickly . . . come, Christ the King, and bring fulfillment, but blow those trumpets loud because we will be up to our elbows in the work of your kingdom!

Just a little more time—but how long?

When Jesus finished saying these things, the crowds were amazed at his teaching, because he taught as one who had authority, and not as their teachers of the law. (Matt. 7:28, 29)

CHAPTER FIFTEEN

Jesus Said!

When you want to make a point, you point to the most competent source. When you want to win an argument, you argue from the strongest position. When you fight a battle, you seek the most strategic location. And when you want your way, you call upon the greatest authority to back you up!

The time had come for me to leave the people at St. John's in Iowa and begin shepherding the people at Peace in Washington State. This was not an easy transition. To make leaving even more difficult, I was leaving behind my family. Although only temporary, this was the most traumatic of all. Washington is a long way from Iowa, and the phone is a poor substitute for hugs and kisses!

The children reacted to this separation and transition in fascinating ways. Much more fascinating to look back on than to go through! I remember one phone conversation with Sara in which she relayed a frustrating example. I laughed—you probably will, too—Sara did not!

Mikal Soo has never been an easy child to put to bed at night. She is also difficult to get up in the morning. I am sure the two are connected, but knowing this has not proved helpful at either end. Every night is a dramatic production that ends up somewhere between tragedy and comedy. Every good stage production has all the proper elements: staging, directing, choreographing, and all the proper parts: plot, characters, climax. And every night with Mikal Soo . . .

"I'm not tired."

"You have to sleep so you can wake up early tomorrow."

"I'm thirsty."

"Here is a drink of water."

"I have to go potty."

"Go!"

"I can't reach the light."

"I'll be right there."

"I'm hungry."

"Eat this cracker."

"I'm hot."

"Take off your pajamas."

"I'm scared."

"You don't have to worry, we are here to take care of you."

"I want the light on."

"Fine!"

"I can't reach the light."

"Coming!"

"I want my door closed."

"Close it!"

"I want my door open."

The sound you are hearing probably resembles a pot on the stove ready to boil off the lid. Does the lid blow? Sometimes!

This nightly production wears upon one's patience, but with the two of us tag teaming we usually survive with minor burns. But then one of the team left the state. One night, Mikal Soo improvised her lines, and it is this act I share with you.

The production started in the usual way and the actors played their parts. Each line was delivered as rehearsed and the same as in previous performances. Every excuse was dealt with, each attempt was thwarted, every move was countered; but then Mikal Soo pioneered new territory!

"Mikal Soo, who told you that you could get out of bed?"

"Daddy said—"

"Daddy is two thousand miles away. He never said such a thing!" (As far as reported to me, no further comment about Daddy being two thousand miles away was added.)

There was a momentary pause from the top of the stairs, and then it came. "Jesus said!"

When you want to make a point, you point to the most competent source. When you want to win an argument, you argue from the strongest position. When you fight a battle, you seek the most strategic location. And, when you want your way, you call upon the greatest authority to back you up!

Mikal Soo went right to the top. Daddy is a pretty high authority in her eyes, but even she realized there is a higher authority. She realized there is an authority higher than Mom's or Dad's, and when you want your way—she went right to the top—Jesus!

Yes, she was wrong in her use of this authority. Yes, she was going against the greatest authority by going against her mother. Yes, she was using this authority to accomplish her purposes and to suit her needs. Yes, but so do we!

Jesus Christ and His holy Word are the greatest authority, but how often do we only look to this authority when we want our own way? How often do we twist and turn the truth to suit our own purposes? How often do we ignore this authority until the time we can get something for ourselves by referring to it? How often?

Authority is a wonderful thing when it suits our purposes, but what happens when it pricks our consciences? Authority is useful when it protects our interests, but what happens when it cramps our lifestyles? Authority is a powerful weapon, but what happens when it backfires? We love the policeman who is protecting our lives and property, but we mutter obscenities when he tickets us. We are thankful when the roads are smooth, the hungry fed, the homeless sheltered, the naked clothed, the sickly strengthened, but we gripe and complain on April 15. We love God and His Word, His Son and His authority, but we are shocked when the sword cuts too close to home.

Authority does not exist to accomplish our purposes. Authority exists to accomplish God's purpose and to carry out His plan. Simple enough, but what happens when the Word becomes personal? Authority is too black and white for us. If God is the ultimate authority then we are not! If Jesus is God's Son, then what He says goes, all the time, in all circumstances. If God's Word is the source and norm of all truth, then we do not have the right to pick and chose what we want to be truth.

This makes us feel uncomfortable. Give up authority, give over control, place reliance upon—too personal! But it is only when we are stripped bare that we see our infection. Only when our perceived mantle of authority is removed do we see the helplessness. Only when the mask is taken away do we see the lost sinner. And only God, by the authority of His Law, can strip away the layers and show us what we are. Not much to look at!

Only God can show us what we are, but it is also true that only God can show us who He wants us to be. Only God can take the revealed wretch and make a new creature. Only God can do this, but such a price.

We are called upon to give up the authority we *think* we have, Christ was called upon to give up the authority He actually had. All authority in heaven and Earth was His, and He laid it aside to become a man. He put on our skin and walked through the mess of our world. He even walked to the cross. The God who alone could strip us bare took all the layers of our wretchedness and laid them upon His Son. And His precious blood washed it away.

New creatures—recreated, restored, redeemed, renewed, released from the power of sin, death, and the devil—placed under the One Authority.

But His burden is light. Often we chafe at the picture of being subservient. We are irritated by the idea of someone telling us what to do and how to act. We are trained to be independent, self-supporting, our own person. So we bump into His authority. But His burden is light.

He rescued us from the slavery to sin and placed us under a new authority—His authority. Purge the worldly picture of authority from your mind and see the picture Christ paints. Servants, but also sons. Slaves, but members of the family of God. Under authority, but perfect authority founded in perfect love.

Jesus said! Yes, He did and does, but a different picture of authority than the world paints. A strange authority. Giving up a throne for a manger. Giving up a royal scepter for a carpenter's hammer. Giving up a place of perfection for a place in need of forgiveness. Giving up a crown of glory for a crown of thorns. Giving up life in order to bestow life on those who deserve death. Why? Why would the Ultimate Authority follow such a path? Why would this amazing grace be lavished upon us? How many times have perplexed people looked at you and wondered, out loud, how anyone could believe such nonsense? And how did you answer?

"Jesus said . . ."

He who testifies to these things says, "Yes, I am coming soon." Amen. Come, Lord Jesus. The grace of the Lord Jesus be with God's people. Amen. (Rev. 22:20, 21)

CHAPTER SIXTEEN

In His Time

Timing is everything. Of course, when we say this we mean my timing is everything. Other timing is off the mark—too early, too late—not good timing. And then there is God's timing! Is there anything more frustrating than God's timing? Is there anything more confusing? Is there anything more puzzling, more maddening?

God's timing is off! What I really mean is God's timing does not coincide with my timing. I suppose you would tell me that it is my timing that is off and God's is right on. Well, maybe, but how do you feel when God's timing does not take into consideration your plans? How do you react when your carefully laid out agenda is trashed by God's order? What are your thoughts when your plans are thrown into disarray by God's inhuman timing? See? God's timing is off!

I remember the joy and excitement when we discovered—with the doctor's help—that Sara was pregnant. Our first child was on the way just like we had planned. Due on

October 31—no, not Halloween, Reformation Day! I'm a Lutheran pastor; this was obviously a sign from God!

So much to do! So many decisions to make. Better work baby furniture into the budget. Speaking of budgets, what about Sara's job? What about diapers and formula? What about college? When I went to the bank to start a savings account for our new baby, they asked me for a social security number.

"Well, the baby isn't exactly born yet."

"First one, right?"

"Yep!"

Of course, I had to clear my calendar for October 31. Reformation Day is a big day at the church, so I wanted to make sure I was free. I convinced everyone we would have a special service on November 1, All Saints' Day, instead. I would be a little tired, but it would be OK!

Preparations were made. Furniture was bought. Budgets were adjusted. Names were tentatively chosen. Schedules were cleared. We were ready!

October 30: "How do you feel honey?"

"The same."

October 31 AM: "How do you feel honey?"

"The same."

October 31 noon: "Any contractions?"

"No."

October 31 PM: "Should I get the suitcase?"

"Shut up."

November 1: Nothing.

November 3: Nothing.

November 7: Still nothing. Off to the doctor.

Everything is fine; everything is normal—at least with the baby! If nothing happens in the next week, it's off to the hospital to induce labor.

November 9: Nothing.

November 11: Nothing.

November 13: "If one more person asks me when the baby is coming . . ."

November 14: Nothing. Off to the hospital.

Medical science will now fix this timing problem. A little juice from the IV bag and presto, a baby, right? Wrong! All day long, drip, drip, drip.

"Anything yet?"

"Nothing."

Drip, drip, drip. "Hey, the monitor jumped!"

"I burped."

Drip, drip, drip. "Honey, you should read this article on deer hunting!"

"Shut up!"

"Well," says the doctor, "today is not the day. (I had that figured out!) May as well go home and we will plan on seeing you a week from today, unless, of course, nature takes its course."

Disappointed? Yes! We stopped at the local pizza joint on the way home. Sara got more contractions from the pepperoni than the IV!

Another week to go. Tears, frustrations, messed up plans—very funny, God!

Another week—no contractions. The pastor has a funeral on the twenty-first. Oh, well, what's another day? Back to, drip, drip, drip. Back to the deer-hunting book.

Back to: "Feel anything yet?"

"No."

"Are you sure . . . never mind!"

Drip, drip, drip, all day long—nothing. The doctors were not so cavalier in their attitudes this time. They seemed a little worried. Not about the baby. They seemed worried about Thanksgiving Day being two days away and the possibility of their feasting being interrupted by a hospital call! This is, after all, a small town hospital and there are only so many doctors to go around.

The authoritative word is spoken: "We are keeping your wife overnight, and this baby *will* be born tomorrow, no matter what!" And that was that!

November 23: Twenty three days overdue, Nathaniel David Pulse showed up right on time—God's time!

In His time, God accomplishes all manner of things, but only in His time. We try to change the schedule. We try to reorder the plan. We try bribery: "God, if You do this when I want it done, I will . . ." We try threats: "God, if this does not happen by such and such a time, I will never . . ." We try con-artistry: "I love You, God, and I promise to serve You and You alone. So, I know You will see things my way and . . ." We try and we try and God still accomplishes all manner of things, but only in His time.

How often have we tried to impose our finite scheduling, our timing, upon the infinite, timeless Creator? We struggle with the possibility of a world being created in six days so we impose "scientific" reckoning upon the Creator. We are confused as to why a loving God would wait thousands of years to patch up a sinful creation, so we assume a distant, unloving, "supreme being." We are frustrated with the waiting game as we look to the Second Coming of our Lord, so we give Him due dates. And He will come—in His time.

In His time He created a perfect world—six days according to His Book. In His time He sent His Son to recreate the creation we messed up. Paul says in Romans, "You see, at just the right time, when we were still powerless,

Christ died for the ungodly" (Rom. 5:6). At just the right time—God's time. In His time.

But, we still struggle with His timing. We have resolved ourselves, more or less, to His past timing, but His present and future timing cause us great concern. Why doesn't God take care of the problems in our world now? Why doesn't God send His Only Begotten back so we can leave this strange and foreign land and go home? In His time. . . .

So we wait. Every time we try to guess, every time we jump to conclusions, every time we set a due date, we end up disappointed. True, God tells us Christ is coming back. In fact, He says soon! What does that mean? In human timing it means during the next disaster or before the dinner bell. According to God's plan it means in His time!

You Can Tell They're Getting Older

Introduction

A nd so they grow up. They get bigger, taller, faster, and smarter. They get older than you expect children (at least your children) would ever get. They learn things, some bad things, but mostly good. They begin to look at the world differently. They discover truths and laws, responsibilities and consequences. Their eyes see the world we live in differently. They smell and taste and feel the same environment we do differently.

This is what makes children so fascinating to me. How do they live in the same reality and experience it in such a foreign way? The truth is, I'm envious! I would love to see things through the eyes of a child again. I long to experience our world without the jaundiced coloring I have acquired as an adult. I want to know the joy! I want the unbridled joy of a child as I walk through this joyless landscape, and I despair in thinking this joy may be unattainable.

God gave me children as a blessing, but also for a reason. Actually, I believe God gave me children for several reasons. One reason is the opportunity to raise them to live in His grace and walk in His paths. Another reason is the beautiful example of what it is like to live in His joy. Through my children I have a glimpse of what this joy is all about. Through my children I am privileged to observe the realities of God's joy in the midst of man's despair. Through my children. And God calls me His child!

God calls us His children. Why doesn't God call us His adults? Maybe because He does not want us to walk around with world-stained, adult eyes. Maybe He wants us to see as a child. Maybe it is the joy He wants us to experience, and He knows, as an adult, we just might miss it. Maybe, but God does call us His children, and He wants us to have the joy that comes through a child-like faith and a child-like perspective of His kingdom.

I am convinced that God's goal of child-likeness for us would be impossible without the example of children. So as they grow older I see them learn. I see them come to understand. I see their wide-eyed wonderment at the everyday. I see the change, but I fear the day they go "backward" and become adults. I pray they never lose their sense of joy as their sight is colored by the world. Still, they do grow up, and, you can tell they're getting older when . . .

*Then the mother of Zebedee's sons came to Jesus
with her sons and, kneeling down, asked a favor of
him. "What is it you want?" he asked. She said,
"Grant that one of these two sons of mine may sit
on your right and the other at your left in your kingdom." "You don't know what you are asking," Jesus
said to them. "Can you drink the cup I am going to
drink?" "We can," they answered. Jesus said to
them, "You will indeed drink from my cup, but to
sit at my right or left is not for me to grant. These
places belong to those for whom they have been prepared by my Father." When the ten heard this, they
were indignant with the two brothers. Jesus called
them together and said, "You know that the rulers
of the Gentiles lord it over them, and their high of-
ficials exercise authority over them. Not so with you.
Instead, whoever wants to become great among you
must be your servant, and whoever wants to be
first must be your slave—just as the Son of Man
did not come to be served, but to serve, and to give
his life as a ransom for many." (Matt. 20:20–28)*

The Princess of Plugging Your Nose

Some time ago, as we journeyed down the rural roads of the state of Iowa on our family vacation, we drove down a section of highway known for its many cattle yards. Having grown up in this environment, the fragrant smell brought back many memories, some bad, most good. As my mind wandered back into time, the odor wandered to the back reaches of the van. Almost in unison our three children broke into the chant of, "Yew!" "Yuck!" "What's that smell?" "That's gross!" "What stinks?" "Close the windows!" Unwilling to leave nostalgia, I immediately responded with the response my father had given me, and probably his father before him: "That's the smell of money!" Of course, this drifted past my children unnoticed. They had already moved into the survival mode.

"Plug your nose!"

My four-year-old daughter, the youngest, decided that this was an opportunity for her to assert her power. "Don't plug your nose until I tell you to!"

Her two brothers were not knuckling under to her control. "I'll plug my nose if I want to!"

She replied, "No, you can't!"

"Oh, yeah? Just watch!"

"You can't plug your nose until I tell you, because . . . because . . . because I'm the Princess of Plugging Your Nose!"

I cannot recall the responses of the boys. Sara and I were too busy losing it in the front seat. The Princess of Plugging Your Nose? All manner of questions was going through our minds. What kind of kingdom is this? Is this a highly sought after position? If she is the princess, are we the king and queen? What is the order of succession?

The one question that occurred to me later was "Why are we humans so eager for positions of power and control?" My daughter may only be four years old, but she exhibited the same urge all people seem to have—the urge to take charge and be in control. Deep within we all want to run the show, and, yet, whenever we run the show, the show runs down. And, if we were to run the show long enough, the show would close.

The One in charge, the One in control, the One who truly knows what to do and when to do it, the One who really knows how to run things is God. He created, He sustains, He is in control—of everything! Tough to swallow. Tougher to acknowledge. Toughest to "let go and let God." Yet this is what the Lord calls upon us to do. Let Him be God. Let Him do what only He can do. Let Him run the show. Stop trying to take over a job description for which we are immensely under-qualified.

History provides a frightening picture of what happens when man tries to run things. From the beginning, in the Garden of Eden when man wanted to be like God, through every age, every era, every time, every day, we find examples of man messing things up. Not necessarily by plan, but nevertheless, the results have always been devastating. From wars and holocausts to family problems and depression, when man tries to take over or even tries to just "help God out," the results are terrible and terrorizing.

The solution? Understand that God is in control. From the beginning His plan has been perfect. Unfortunately, man keeps messing it up. Man messes up, God cleans up. Man breaks down, God fixes up. Man confuses, God clears. Man gets lost, God finds. Even when man destroyed the perfection of God's creation, God had a plan to reconstruct through His Son. By the blood of Christ, God has redeemed, re-created, renewed, restored, and regenerated man. He can do these things because of who He is, not because of who we are! Because He is God, He can create and continue to take care of things. Because we are humans, we often get in the way. And because He loves us, He keeps reminding us of who is who and what is what!

This is God's world. It has been created to run according to His guidance and governance. Even though we have the desire to create our own little kingdoms (Princess of Plugging Your Nose?), the truth is, we only confuse ourselves and those around us. The Creator knows what is best for the created. The Father is the head of His family. It's when we turn things around that the difficulties begin.

"O Jerusalem, Jerusalem, you who kill the prophets and stone those sent to you, how often I have longed to gather your children together, as a hen gathers her chicks under her wings, but you were not willing. Look, your house is left to you desolate. For I tell you, you will not see me again until you say, 'Blessed is he who comes in the name of the Lord.'" (Matt. 23:37–39)

CHAPTER TWO

De-hugged!

I have the joy and privilege to be the pastor where my children go to school. Because we have a parochial school, my children are on the same piece of property as their father five days out of the week. Not everyone has this blessing—not everyone wants it! I do, and it is a great joy for me.

Last year, as I walked over to the school building, I saw my youngest son, Jonathan, in the office being patched up. He had fallen on the rocks, was scraped, and required the usual bandage and hug. Following these treatments, he walked out of the office and there I was—Dad. He came right over to tell me what had happened and to receive condolences, concerns, and care. I checked him out, brushed off imaginary dirt, gave him words of encouragement, bent over to give him a hug, and that was when it happened—*he de-hugged me!*

Just when I went to wrap my arms around him, he turned his shoulder to me and de-hugged me. That hurt!

As he pulled away—walked away—I gave it another shot. "How about a hug? How about a slurpie?" (Don't ask!) He just kept on walking! Actually, when I asked about the hug, he half-stopped, started to turn, wanted to return, but then he thought better and just kept going. *Ouch!*

He wanted the customary comfort from his father, but there were witnesses. After all, he wasn't a kid anymore. He was grown up—he was in the first grade! There were preschoolers and kindergartners looking up to him. He had to "protect the rep." And, there I stood, stupid. There I was, struck dumber than normal. I was crushed! My little boy didn't need me anymore. Other things in life were more important than what I had to offer as a daddy. Embarrassment was not worth the embrace. Kidding was not worth the kiss. The hassle was not worth the hug. *It nearly broke my heart!* Fortunately, the school nurse bandaged my pride, and I limped through the rest of the day.

Have you ever been de-hugged? Have you ever had your love, kindness, and concern rejected by one of your children? Painful, isn't it? Have you ever wondered how our heavenly Father feels when we de-hug Him?

The children of God have a rather long history of turning their backs on the One who loves them the most. The children of God are constantly and consistently pushing away from the loving embrace of their perfect Father. I am not exactly sure what causes this response to God's love, but it is a common response. Perhaps it is driven by embarrassment, or fear, or pride, or independence, or plain stupidity; whatever, in effect it "de-hugs" God!

How foolish to de-hug the One who loved us so much He gave His Only Begotten. How amazing to de-hug the One who gave His most Beloved to rescue and redeem fallen mankind. How can we turn our back on the One who faced the nightmare of death on a cross to restore and return us to His family? I wonder how our Father in heaven feels when we walk away?

I know my son and I know how much that hug meant to him. I know his needs and I know he needed the love I wanted to pour out, but he walked away.

God says, "I know my children and I know how much they need My blessings and love. I know their needs—I have met their greatest need. I have so much more to pour out. My arms reach out to them every day in every way, but, so often they stay just beyond My reach."

I wonder if it just about breaks God's heart?

Dear friends, let us love one another, for love comes from God. Everyone who loves has been born of God and knows God. Whoever does not love does not know God, because God is love. (1 John 4:7, 8)

CHAPTER THREE

That's Not Hard to Know!

Both sides of our family live in Iowa. This requires annual pilgrimages east to visit. However, there is more to a pilgrimage than the going, there is also the returning, and this is often the most difficult part of the journey. Difficult, because parents and children are tired. Difficult, because the type and level of emotion is radically different. Difficult, because the atmosphere of anticipation is not so high and exciting.

During a recent return voyage from Iowa, we stopped at a truck stop to look for an Iowa key chain (another story for another time). We had just begun the trip back a few hours earlier and the emotion of leaving family was still raw. Tears flowed for the smallest of reasons. As we pulled into the truck stop and parked our van, my wife was overcome with one of these waves of emotion, and she turned to the nearest and oldest child and said, "Nathan, your grandparents love you a lot!"

Nathan looked at his mother with a perplexed expression on his face and said, "That's not hard to know." He said it so matter-of-fact-like. He said it with absolute confidence. He said it as if there were no room for discussion. There was no doubt in his mind. The only question he seemed to have was: This is so obvious why must we bring it up? There are key chains to buy!

Isn't it amazing? In a day when we spend hours in counseling and therapy to determine whether or not we are loved, there was no doubt in his mind. In a day and age when one often needs a scorecard to follow one's family tree, he knew right where he was planted. In a day and age—our day and age—when we question the motives of those who want to be close to us, Nathan saw no hidden agendas, no loopholes, no problems. That's not hard to know!

I know it is often difficult and sometimes unsafe to trust the human race. It is a sad but true condition of our race. The saddest truth, however, is that we allow the lack of trust in ourselves to invade our trust in our God. So often we allow the lack of love for one another serve as the barometer of God's love for us. This is a sad condition because it does not accurately reflect the way our Lord and God views us.

God loves us! Perfectly, unconditionally, no strings attached, no payments to be made, no requirements to first be met—God loves us. How can we be so sure? How can we know? Look, examine, see the evidence. God sent His Son when we were unlovable. He gave up the most Beloved to Him in order to rescue and redeem the most rebellious toward Him. This is love—His love for us. There is no other explanation that fits the evidence. None!

There is more, more evidence of the truth concerning God's love for you and me. God grants forgiveness and salvation. God walks with us, protecting, guiding, nurturing. God comforts, gives peace, pours out joy. God provides for our every need. I could go on and on, and on and on (some would say it is my occupation!), but enough has been said to prove the point—God loves us!

What a joy it is to live each day in the knowledge of His love. How comforting and comfortable to be His beloved child. How reassuring to never fear rejection. How amazing and joyful to hear the words, "God loves you," and be able to respond, "That's not hard to know!"

*I want to know Christ and the power of his resur-
rection and the fellowship of sharing in his sufferings, becoming like him in his death, and so,
somehow, to attain to the resurrection from the dead.
Not that I have already obtained all this, or have
already been made perfect, but I press on to take
hold of that for which Christ Jesus took hold of me.
Brothers, I do not consider myself yet to have taken
hold of it. But one thing I do: Forgetting what is behind and straining toward what is ahead, I press
on toward the goal to win the prize for which God
has called me heavenward in Christ Jesus. (Phil.
3:10–14)*

CHAPTER FOUR

Still a Winner

The race was on! We pulled into the parking lot, the car went into park, the doors flew open, and the race was on! Three children exploded from the back seat and hit the ground running. The race to school was on! I must tell you, this kind of behavior is frowned upon. Running is discouraged; walking is encouraged. Still, off they raced!

Everyone wanted to be first. First one out of the car, first one to the door, first one in the door of the school building. Competition—gotta win! But not everyone can be first. Not everyone can cross the finish line together. Someone must come in last. In this case, the odds are against Mikal Soo. She is the youngest. She is the smallest. She has the shortest legs. She is the slowest. The only way she is going to beat anyone to the door is to cross-body block one of her brothers. Of course, then she would only come in second.

Across the parking lot, up the sidewalk to the front door they sprint, and, as expected, Mikal Soo is last. As she bursts through the front doors, breathless, she proclaims to the group of coffee-hugging teachers, "I'm still a winner!" And off to class she waltzes.

Still a winner! Obviously, Mikal Soo does not suffer from a lack of self-confidence. In fact, her self-esteem measurements may be off the chart, but in a world without the Olympic Games, without sports, in a world without a win-at-all-costs attitude, in other words, in God's world, in God's kingdom, she is right.

This is a reality with which our world struggles, but the truth is not the one who dies with the most toys, wins. The truth is the one who dies with the most toys still dies! This reality is the reason God fills His Word with more references to finishing the race than winning the race. The one who finishes the race is still a winner! The goal is not to be the first one to the gates of heaven. The goal is to be at the gates of heaven—first, second, last—but at the gates!

Saint Paul spends a great deal of time speaking of the running of the race, and his encouragement is to cross the finish line—*finish*! All who finish, first, second, last, are winners! I find this encouraging because I have never considered myself to be much of a sprinter. Physically or spiritually, sprinting is not my strength. Of course, this is true of all mankind. Some start off slow, others wear out before the race is done, still others fall by the wayside because of the refreshment stands—not one of us would even finish, first, second, or last, if we did not have help. Thank God we have help!

God, who sent His Son to put us in the race, also sent His Spirit to help us finish the race. By the blood of Christ we are made the children of God and are in the race lineup.

By the power of the Spirit we run the race of faith with strength, perseverance, and endurance, with eyes focused on the finish line. God's Son, God's Spirit—our help to run the race comes from the Lord!

What a comfort and encouragement this is, because without such help we are losers. No medal ceremony for any of us. No cheering cloud of witnesses. No heavenly cross-national anthems. No prize, no reward, no mansion. But, because God has placed us in the race through the sacrifice of His Son, and because God does not make us run this race alone, we are still winners!

Your attitude should be the same as that of Christ Jesus: Who, being in very nature God, did not consider equality with God something to be grasped, but made himself nothing, taking the very nature of a servant, being made in human likeness. And being found in appearance as a man, he humbled himself and became obedient to death—even death on a cross! Therefore God exalted him to the highest place and gave him the name that is above every name, that at the name of Jesus every knee should bow, in heaven and on earth and under the earth, and every tongue confess that Jesus Christ is Lord, to the glory of God the Father. (Phil. 2:5–11)

CHAPTER FIVE

What's the Word?

I know a word."

The short sentence struck fear into my heart. I could feel my heart rate increase and the blood pressure go up. I did not know whether to respond or run. That dreadful little sentence.

"What's the big deal?" you ask. Let me paint the picture for you. Let me set the stage. It was early morning at the Pulse residence. I was the first one up, and as I stood in front of the bathroom mirror scraping my face, in wandered my four-year-old son, Nathan. He lounged around for awhile watching my facial gyrations, then he spoke: "Daddy, I know a word." I nearly scarred myself! Only four years old and he already knows words—those words! What are they teaching him at preschool? What will the elders at church say?

I calmly laid down the razor, grabbed hold of the bathroom counter with both hands, took a deep breath and asked, "What is it?"

Nathan looked at me, stood up straight and proud, and announced, *discussion.*

As I wiped the spray off the mirror, I asked him if he knew what it meant. He did. I asked him where he had heard it. Some educational TV program. I asked him if he knew how to dial 911—just kidding!

Words are amazing and powerful things. They can dredge up strong emotions. They can create fears, they can calm fears. They can enslave, they can free. Words are powerful! Since words are so powerful, it is important to know how to use them. It is important to know words.

I know a word. It is a word that invokes feelings of peace, joy, comfort, and assurance. It is a word that reminds of mercy, grace, and love. It is a word that names the fulfiller of promises, both temporal and eternal. It is a word that is heard frequently, but it is often misused. The word is *Jesus!*

Think of all the powerful emotions this name, this word, has caused throughout the history of our world. This word has caused people to respond and act in amazing, albeit, not always godly, ways. This word is used to praise and curse. This word is used to worship and swear. At the speaking of this word, people have fallen to their knees while others have drawn swords.

The word is *Jesus*, and at the speaking, one should be reminded of love that is boundless; grace that is endless; mercy that is fathomless. This word should remind us of a Father who gave His most precious gift. It should remind us that we are the undeserving receivers of this gift. It should remind us of why we give gifts. How can we hold back our gifts from those around us when the Father has so graciously, so unselfishly, so abundantly held nothing back from us?

The word is *Jesus*, and no other word has caused so many discussions and stirred so many hearts and irritated so many emotions. I wonder why?

Not only so, but we also rejoice in our sufferings, because we know that suffering produces perseverance; perseverance, character; and, character, hope. And hope does not disappoint us, because God has poured out his love into our hearts by the Holy Spirit, whom he has given us. You see, at just the right time, when we were still powerless, Christ died for the ungodly. Very rarely will anyone die for a righteous man, though for a good man someone might possibly dare to die. But God demonstrates his own love for us in this: While we were still sinners, Chris died for us. (Rom. 5:3–8)

CHAPTER SIX

Pay Attention!

P ay attention when I am talking to you!"
How many times have you said these words? I would imagine they have been uttered toward less than attentive children—your own, your students, your children's children—as you tried to get them to listen carefully, completely, and without distraction. I know there are many times when I have used these words or words similar to them.

There are just too many distractions, and when I am talking I want their complete, undivided attention. Why? Because I want them to hear me. More than that, I want them to hear, understand, and then act according to what I am telling them!

"I am not just talking to entertain myself!"

Are we, as adults, any better? Do we listen better? Do we hear more completely? Do we give our undivided attention? Do we give it to our children?

Mikal Soo has developed a habit that is extremely irritating. Not irritating because it is terrible and wrong, irritating because it brings me face to face with my lack of coming face to face! Let me explain.

As many parents do, when my children talk to me, I listen with only half an ear. Not good! In fact, even when I listen with a "whole ear," I give the impression of half attention because I do not look at the child speaking to me. Mikal Soo does not like to be ignored in any sense of the word. The irritating habit she has developed is to grab my face and force me to look her right in the eye while she delivers her message. I hate that! Of course, it is hard to deny my complete attention when forcibly focused in.

Sometimes it takes a lot to get our attention. Certainly this is true for children. Yes, it is also true of adults. And it is most certainly true of our attention span when it comes to God! We do not listen well to our God. It is not that we are uninterested, it is just that there are many distractions to keep our focus away from Him. I do not think this is a coincidence! Satan knows how to distract us, and the One he most wants us to be distracted from is God!

So, due to our lack of attention, God has to get our attention. Often times we find Him helping us focus in. And, no, it is not always the most pleasant attention-getter. Perhaps He uses trials and tribulations; maybe sufferings and sorrows; maybe betrayal and denial; maybe unhappy and depressing situations. God wants our attention. Why? Because He has some important things He wants to share with us. He has some exciting things to tell. He has some important blessings to point out. Pay attention!

He sent His Son. Jesus paid the price for our sins on the cross. We are forgiven. We have salvation and everlasting life. He is still with us. He is still piling on the blessings. He is still protecting and strengthening. He is still heaping up good stuff for His people. And He wants you to be aware of all these things. Oh, but how difficult it can be to get our attention!

And He tries, and we wonder why God allows these things, and we ponder what this all means, and we complain about His technique; but He gets our attention, and He shares His message, and we find ourselves counting our blessings.

"Pay attention, I am talking to you!"

"You did not choose me, but I chose you and appointed you to go and bear fruit—fruit that will last." (John 15:16a)

CHAPTER SEVEN

A Strange Choice

It always happens between church services. It never fails that something happens, some information is relayed between services that is terribly distracting to the upcoming task—church! Usually, it happens as I prepare to walk down the aisle to welcome and make announcements. Someone has something distressing or distracting to pass along to me, and once it is in my head, it tends to push other things out—such as my name or the name of the church!

One Sunday, over six years ago, the new pastor (me!) had just such an experience. One of the Sunday school teachers came to me with a funny look on her face. She wanted to tell me something about my children. She asked me if we prayed with our hands on top of our heads at the Pulse home? I looked at her quizzically and said, "No, why?"

"Mikal Soo was praying that way at the end of Sunday school, and when I asked her about it, she claimed this was the way you always pray at home! In fact," the teacher continued, "Jonathan backed her up and assured me, absolutely, this was the truth!"

The teacher was having a great time with this news. She seemed to understand that my children were pulling her leg. Still, in her eyes I thought I detected a glimmer of concern. Perhaps she was wondering about this new pastor. After all, what do we really know about him? Maybe he is a little strange. Maybe his children are showing us a reflection of him.

Have you ever wondered what people saw when the looked at John the Baptist? Have you ever wondered what thoughts were going through their minds? Did the people go out to hear the voice of one crying in the wilderness or did they go out to see this weird guy in camel clothes munching on locusts? It is hard to tell, but we are told in Scripture what they saw. More important, we are told in Scripture what they heard: "Repent ye: for the kingdom of heaven is at hand! Prepare ye the way of the Lord" (Matt. 3:2 KJV)

What an interesting messenger for the Messiah. Was he elegant and articulate? We do not know. Was he strange and unusual? The Word says yes! Was he speaking and directing according to God's plan? Again, God's Word is clear—yes!

God has demonstrated an interesting desire to call and use unlikely and unusual people to spread His Word. From Elijah to Hosea, from John the Baptist to the apostle Paul, God is continually sending out His Word through strange people. Even today, those called into God's ministry often appear to be strange choices. But consider this: Which one of us is not a strange choice? Which one of us is worthy? How can the sinful be worthy of the perfect? How can the human be called to proclaim the divine?

Not one of us is worthy. Yet, every one of us is tasked with the spreading of this important message. John the Baptist was chosen to proclaim the coming of Christ to bring forgiveness and salvation to a fallen world. You and I are chosen to proclaim that this is a reality and that the Son of God makes ready for His return.

We are chosen for this task, not because of our righteousness, but because of the righteousness of Christ poured out upon us! Worthy? Only by His blood! Gifted? Only by the Spirit! Prepared? Only by His grace!

A strange choice, indeed. But in His wisdom, God has done many things that seem rather strange to man. On the surface, it may even appear that God does not know what He is doing, but, if you have any doubts, read His Word and see His perfect track record!

Therefore go and make disciples of all nations, baptizing them in the name of the Father and of the Son and of the Holy Spirit, and teaching them to obey everything I have commanded you. And surely I am with you always, to the very end of the age. (Matt: 28:19, 20)

CHAPTER EIGHT

Go!

One day, as we journeyed through Iowa on our vacation, Jonathan, out of the clear blue, said, "When I grow up I'm not going to be one of those 'wish you luck' people."

After a little probing, Jonathan's meaning became clear. He was actually referring to the people who stood around patting the astronauts on the back, wishing them luck as they climbed aboard the most recent space shuttle. What he meant was, when he grew up, he was not going to be one of those people who wished other people luck, he was going to be one of those people on the space shuttle! None of this sitting around while other people have adventures and make history, he was going to be having the adventures and making the history! That's my boy!

It was the same little boy who stood at Mount Rushmore with his family and strongly declared that he, too, was going to be a stone man someday! Jonathan intended to have his own face up on the mountain!

What do you suppose I, as a father, said to my child? "Jonathan, there is no more room on Mount Rushmore for your face." "Jonathan, the odds of you ever being an astronaut are, well, astronomical!" Of course not! These words would have been very inappropriate responses. I appropriately encouraged him.

It is very important to encourage and support the dreams and goals of our children. After all, which one of us can say for certain they will not go where no man has gone before?

Who is responsible to encourage and support the dreams and goals of adult children? In other words, who is it that encourages the children of God to move forward with His plan for them, His mission and commission for His people? One thing I can say to you for certain: *No one has been assigned the task of discouraging God's children from moving forward!*

Did you know that? This job description, or assignment, is not to be found anywhere in God's Word. Rather, God continually challenges us to seek ways, new ways, better ways, to carry His gospel message to the ends of the earth. Instead of limiting, God is always encouraging us to expand our vision, expand our goals, expand our plans, because only in expanding will we begin to see how large God's plan is for us. People seldom think too large. More often, they think far too small.

God says, "Go into the world. . . ." God's people say, "We have never been there before." God says, "Preach the Word to every nation." God's people say, "The door is closed to that nation." God says, "I desire all people to be saved." God's people say, "We are not really sure God wants those people (that person?) in heaven." God is expansive; His people tend to downsize!

The only time God calls upon us to step back and re-think is when our plans are not in accordance with His plans. Yet, even at these times, God does not tell us to stop moving. He tells us to move forward differently.

God's plan for us and His Church is bigger than we would like to admit. Bigger is frightening. Bigger means serious commitment. Bigger means out of our control. God's plan is so big we cannot handle it, not to mention carry it out, without His help.

That's part of His plan too!

We proclaim him, admonishing and teaching everyone with all wisdom, so that we may present everyone perfect in Christ. To this end I labor, struggling with all his energy, which so powerfully works in me. (Col. 1:28, 29)

CHAPTER NINE

I Just Want to Walk Through the Water

I t happened in the back of a pickup truck. When you are a child, the back of a pickup truck can serve many purposes. A little imagination, and it becomes the launching pad for all manner of exciting adventures. The children were in the back of grandpa's pickup with their cousins. They were imagining great things! They were embarking upon magnificent journeys! They were being silly (my "adult-ness" just kick in!).

Today they were playing "Moses." Jonathan had assumed the role of Moses, and, as the assumed (presumed?) leader, he was handing out assignments. Sara happened to be around the corner and witnessed the following: Our daughter was being uncooperative—imagine that! She was not pleased with any of the available roles. As Sara came around the corner, Mikal Soo stomped her little foot and said, "I don't want to be Moses' wife. I don't want to be a soldier. I just want to walk through the water!"

Boy, can I relate to that! Imagine Moses with his staff. He has been talking to God, and you know something big, something important is about to happen—at least you hope so because you can smell the dust from the Egyptian army moving in fast. Suddenly, the water starts to roar and back up. You look out across the Red Sea and walls of water are building on both sides of a path—a wide path—a wide, dry path. Deliverance! A timely rescue! God to the rescue! Let's get out of here!

Then a voice says to you, "As we go through the Red Sea we need to be singing that special song. Will you be one of the song leaders?" "We need someone to organize the march through so no one is trampled." "We need someone to count heads." "Will you please lead your clan through?" "We need a strong leader to bring up the rear." And what do you say? "Hey! I just want to walk through the water!" "I do not want a job. I do not want responsibilities. I do not want a challenge. Just let me walk through the water!"

And, so, the Church of God sputters and putters along.

Boy, can I relate to that! I'm not complaining about the members of the family of God; I'm confessing about me! There are many days when I just want to walk through the water. I do not want the extra challenges. I do not want the added responsibilities. I do not even want the opportunities. Just let me putter along in a comfortable way, in a comfortable zone. Just let me walk through the water.

Easy—just give me easy! A tempting and comfortable thought, isn't it? But God does not call His children to easy. He does not promise comfortable. God never asks us to just walk through the water. There is too much at stake! There is too much to do!

The God who sent His Son to a cross to rescue all mankind calls His Church to reach all mankind. The God who showed infinite and amazing love to all people calls His Church to love likewise. The God who pours out grace and mercy in quantities never experienced before or after calls His Church to spread this abundance across our globe. Walk through the water? Yes! Just walk through the water? No!

The Church of God is not to sputter and putter. The Church of God is to zoom and boom! Zoom out into the world and boom out the beautiful message of God's redeeming love and everlasting grace!

Just walk through the water? Not hardly!

Your word is a lamp to my feet and a light for my path. (Ps. 119:105)

CHAPTER TEN

Do You Hear What I'm Saying?

As I looked out the window, I saw what I did not want to see. I saw my child, my son, doing things I did not want him to do. I saw Nathan acting in ways I did not want him to act. In fact, I raised him better than that! (An old phrase my parents used with me that never made sense—until now!) Oh, it really wasn't anything that terrible. Maiming and murder were not involved. Vandalism and destruction were not the issue. Wholesale carnage and insider trading were not taking place. Still, I raised him better than that!

Nathan was outside at our church's daycare. He was playing around with the other children, but he was treating some of the smaller children in a mean way. He was irritating them on purpose and laughing about it. I know this falls a little short of gang activity and drug use, still, visions of him growing up to be a talk show host started flashing through my head, and we frown on this kind of behavior at home! So, fulfilling my role as father, I tapped loudly on the window to get Nathan's attention, then I mouthed the words, "Nathan, behave yourself!" (Or something like that!)

Well, Nathan looked at me through the glass, saw my lips move, saw my body language, saw the look in my eye, and immediately interpreted my words and responded appropriately. He said, "I love you, too, Daddy!"

What do you do? How do you respond? I retreated and contemplated what had just taken place. I delivered a message but Nathan received something completely different. I was working on the tough love approach, and Nathan was picking up warm fuzzies!

Communication is a tricky thing. Words do not always deliver the message intended. We say one thing and people hear another. And if we have trouble communicating with those who are in the same realm, on the same plane, how much more troubling is this concerning communication from our God?

Do we really hear what God is saying? Or, do we hear what we want Him to say? One is honest and convicting, the other is comfortable and convenient. While we may feel very good about believing that whatever we say, think, do, or believe is God's will and pleases Him; if it is not the truth, it is a very dangerous feeling! If it is not the truth, we are treading on the thin ice of humanistic theology, which is the ultimate oxymoron!

So, how do we know what God is saying? How can we be sure we are hearing correctly? Becoming one with the universe is not going to cut it since the universe is filled with sin and no longer represents its Creator accurately. The world around us only helps us to hear what we want to hear, not what God is trying to communicate. The only way to know what God is saying is to listen to Him in the way He has chosen to speak to us—His Word—the Bible!

God has revealed His message to man through the Bible. It is in this Holy Book we read of His plan of salvation for all people. The pages of this Book reveal the lengthy path God led His people down until they were properly ready for the coming of His Son. This Book tells of Christ, of the need for His sacrifice, of the effect of His blood shedding, of His resurrection from the grave, of His ascent into heaven, of His work to open the gates of heaven to all believers. The pages of Scripture tell of the saving gospel message of Jesus Christ.

These pages also tell us that God does not wink His eye at sin. He does not condone or turn His head when we do wrong. He makes it clear there is a right and a wrong, and what is right is *right* and what is wrong is *wrong*! These are not negotiable commodities. Time, culture, situation, stature, position, or pressure does not change the message of truth. God tells us that sin is a serious issue, so serious He had to rescue us from that which we could not save ourselves. So serious, He delivered His own Son as the sacrifice to rescue us from sin and restore us to new life. Sin is a serious truth and required serious action from God.

Hearing what God has to tell us is not easy—not as long as we listen to our own desires or the corrupt voice of our world. It is always easier to hear what we want to hear, but it really does us no good. God's message to us is intense and serious, but it is also loving and kind. Listen carefully to what He is really saying!

Therefore, just as sin entered the world through one man, and death through sin, and in this way death came to all men, because all sinned . . . But the gift is not like the trespass. For if the many died by the trespass of the one man, how much more did God's grace and the gift that came by the grace of the one man, Jesus Christ, overflow to the many! (Rom. 5:12, 15)

CHAPTER ELEVEN

Stuck in the Middle

One day a few years back the children were playing in the house. I am sure it must have been raining outside (what are the odds of that in the great Northwest?). They were playing what we called cops and robbers when I was growing up. I suppose it was "law enforcement officers and perpetrators" because my children are much more sophisticated than I was at their age (or any age for that matter). Anyway, Mikal Soo had taken on the role of law enforcement agent and was chasing the felons through the house. As they stormed by me, Mikal Soo skidded to a halt, and in a very tough, squeaky voice she hollered, "Stop in the middle of the law!"

I cracked up! There was something in the demanding tone of her voice and her misspoken words that wiped me out. Then when I calmed down, it occurred to me there was a sermon illustration here somewhere.

"Stop in the middle of the law!"

Isn't this what we as God's people do? God gave us His Law in order to prepare us for His beautiful gospel message. He gave us His Law so that we would see our sins and our inability to deal with them and our need for His love, grace, and mercy. He gave us His Law so we would better understand the love of His gospel, and somewhere along the way, we get stuck right in the middle!

Stuck in the middle of the Law. This is not—never was—God's intention for His people. The Law is to show the need for the gospel and give us a clear picture of how God wants us to live as His gospel people—and we get stuck, right in the middle of the Law!

What a tragedy: To be stuck in the middle of the Law when there is such love, mercy and grace! Think about it: "I know Jesus died on the cross to forgive all sin—except for that certain one I did." *Stuck!* "I know I am a sinner and need to get my act together, but I am not as bad as other people." *Stuck!* "I know God has a purpose and plan for each one of His children, but that does not mean me." *Stuck!* "Look at all the terrible things that are happening in your life. God must be angry with you." *Stuck!* Stuck right in the middle of the Law. Stuck, stranded short of the freeing gospel of Jesus Christ. Stuck right where God does not want you to be!

God showed us great love and mercy in His Son. God's love and mercy as seen in Jesus is complete. It is enough. It is totally sufficient. It does not leave you stuck or stranded anywhere! Christ's actions on the cross, on our behalf, bring complete freedom from the accusations of the Law. Complete freedom—no ifs, ands, or buts! No strings, no escape clauses, no fine print—complete freedom. Complete freedom, complete forgiveness, complete salvation. *Complete!*

Stuck in the middle of the Law? No! Remember, God's rescue and restoration are complete. We have been delivered from the accusing nature of the Law completely. *Unstuck!*

In the past God spoke to our forefathers through the prophets at many times and in various ways, but in these last days he has spoken to us by his Son, whom he appointed heir of all things, and through whom he made the universe. (Heb. 1:1, 2)

All Clear!

W e were traveling down the road early one morning. I was driving the children to school. It was
one of those foggy mornings down by the water,
but the day promised to be bright and sunny. As we drove
along through the murky, cloudy mist, we suddenly, sur-
prisingly broke through the fog into a bright, brilliant clearing. The sun was shining, reflecting off the water. Everything
was, at least for that brief moment, crystal clear. Then we
drove back into the fog again. Nothing unusual, nothing
uncommon about this experience, at least not in the Northwest. The reaction from the back seat is what stood out.

The two boys, almost in unison, exclaimed, "Daddy, we
just had an epiphany moment!"

Well, I know what an epiphany moment is, but I wasn't
so sure the boys had a clue, so I asked. I was wrong! They
knew exactly what an epiphany moment was. They told
me it is when something that is unclear suddenly becomes
clear. Suddenly you can see, you get the point, something

is revealed that was hidden. Just like driving through the fog into the bright light. They knew! They learned it from the associate pastor at chapel.

I had never considered leaving the fog for sunlight as an epiphany moment, but it did fit the definition. It makes me wonder if I am missing other epiphany moments as I journey through this life. It makes me wonder if maybe I am missing some of the epiphany moments God sets up for my education and edification. That concerns me! After all, if God is talking, if God is revealing, if God is leading, I sure do not want to be out to lunch!

We spend a great deal of time trying to discern God's will in this situation or that. People are always asking, "What is God doing?" "Why is God doing?" "Why isn't God doing?" "How do I know the what and the why?" "Where do I fit in?" We want to know. We struggle terribly in not knowing. How ironic it would be to desperately search for God's direction as we stand under His street signs.

What's the answer? How do we experience the epiphany? We inquire of God's will and we need to know! There is no perfect, and, certainly no easy answer, to this question. The place to start is the ultimate will of God. This we know: The ultimate will of God is that all men would be saved. God desires that each and every man, woman, and child would know His big epiphany—Jesus—and be part of His kingdom. This is the reason Christ came into our world; this is why He went to the cross; this is why He laid down His life; this is why He shed His blood; this is why the gates of heaven are open before us. No secret here— God loves us so much, He sent His Son so that we might be His children. The ultimate will of God.

God also tells us some of the things He desires for His children. He says, "Read and study My Word." "Pray—a lot!" "Worship with your fellow believers." "Hang out with Christians." "Reach out with My epiphanied gospel message." "Dedicate yourself to My things—the things of God!" This is God's will for His children. Walk the paths of God, immersed in the things of God.

Then, then, as you grow in your faith and understanding, the details of God's will for you will become clear. Then the light will come on. Then you will begin to notice and recognize the epiphany moments He sets up for you. The way to know God's will and to see the revelations He gives us is to be immersed in the things of God.

There really should be nothing astonishing to us in all of this. We should already know. We know that if we want to understand our opponent we need to "get into his head." We know that if we want to appreciate our neighbor we should walk in his shoes (moccasins). We know that if we want to learn the language, the culture, the society of another land we need to go and live there for a time.

And, if you want to know God, if you want to understand His will, if you want to see His epiphanies, then live in His house, spend time with His children, read His writings, and spend a lot of time in private conversation with Him. I am sure there are several epiphanies just waiting!

For you were once darkness, but now you are light in the Lord. Live as children of light (for the fruit of the light consists in all goodness, righteousness and truth) and find out what pleases the Lord. Have nothing to do with the fruitless deeds of darkness, but rather expose them. For it is shameful even to mention what the disobedient do in secret. But everything exposed by the light becomes visible, for it is light that makes everything visible. This is why it is said: "Wake up, O sleeper, rise from the dead, and Christ will shine on you." (Eph. 5:8–14)

CHAPTER THIRTEEN

Hold On to the Light

How important is it for you to be able to see where you are going? I suppose it has a lot to do with what you are doing. Are you driving or riding? Directing or following? Awake or asleep? These are all factors that determine the level of urgency of being able to see where you are going.

On vacation in South Dakota the family went spelunking. Well, actually, we took a cave tour. I love caves! I am certain, however, each member of my family does not share my love for dark, wet, cold, and deep. (I'm referring to the climate of caves, not the Northwest!) The reason I am certain not everyone in my family shares this enthusiasm is the response Jonathan had in going into a cave. He was not going to do it! Of course, in true little-boy fashion, he did not make this clear until we were down at the bottom of the shaft walking into the entrance—too late!

Apparently, this was not an uncommon reaction because the guide knew exactly what to do. She knelt down in front of Jonathan and said, "Jonathan, I need your help on this tour. I have this flashlight I want you to carry and use if we need to see where we are going." Now, while this technique never works for parents, the park service has it tuned to perfection. Jonathan's eyes lighted up, his back stiffened up, his attitude straightened up, and off we went!

I thought Jonathan came around because he was given a job to do. I was wrong! The truth is, Jonathan came around because he was given a light! He was not about to enter into the dark unknown unless he had some guidance, something to give him light. As I reflect on this (no pun intended), I think Jonathan was very wise.

Too often, we embark upon journeys without the proper "light." Too often, we try to go forward without a clue. Too often, we go where we cannot see, and we take no precautions to assure we will not walk off a cliff! We seem to want no guidance. We would rather thump and bump our heads and hearts than to accept direction. So off we go, and soon all our fears and tears are realized. Off we go into the dark unknown and before long our cares and the snares overwhelm us. And it doesn't have to be like that! It isn't supposed to be like that!

As difficult as it is to accept, the truth is, we need guidance. The truth is we need light. The truth is, God has provided us with His Truth. God has given us His Light—the Light of His Word. This Light reveals the path. This Light directs us on a journey that is God-pleasing and people-safe. This Light illumines the obstacles, the pitfalls, and the snares that cause the painful scrapes and bruises of life.

First, however, the Light of God's Word reveals the Light of God's grace. First, it shows the mercy God has for mankind. First, it reveals the fathomless love a Creator has for His workmanship. First, it shows us our sin, then it shows the sinless One, Jesus Christ. He is the One who gives direction and guidance to the lost. He is the One who provides for the wanderer. He is the One who turns the aimless. He is the One, the only true Light.

How important is it for you to be able to see where you are going? As Jonathan would tell you, "If you want to see where you are going, hold on to the light!"

But because of his great love for us, God, who is rich in mercy, made us alive with Christ even when we were dead in transgressions—it is by grace you have been saved. (Eph. 2:4, 5)

CHAPTER FOURTEEN

Anything I Want

I wish my teacher would let me do what I want to do!" So proclaimed my son Nathan as he climbed in the car after school one day. Now, with most fourth graders, you might think he wants more recess time or a longer lunch or P.E. Not Nathan! Actually, he wanted the teacher to give him more time to read. He thought it was a great injustice to be forced to move on to another subject when the book was just getting good.

Harmless stuff, but I couldn't help but hear myself and other adults as we voice our own frustrations concerning those in authority over us. "I wish the patrolman would let me drive as fast as I want. I know my abilities!" "I wish the boss would recognize my talents and let me work on the project of my choice." "I wish the government would stop governing where I do not need it." And, of course, the ultimate: "I wish God would let me do what I want to do!"

This is far from harmless. In fact, it is downright dangerous because we tend to act upon our desires. In an effort to get the Almighty to fall in line with our wishes, we change God. In reality, what we attempt to do is re-create God in our own image. We attempt to make Him how He "should be," how we want Him to be. Our desire is to make a god that fits us as we see us.

The problem is that we do not always see us as we are. Unfortunate, but true! This is the reason our re-created god always comes up short. We find that "god in our image" is too shallow and ultimately useless when the realities of our world knock on the door. This is the house built on the sand. A nice, beach-side cottage with a great view, personally chosen and created. But then the winds of change start to rise and the storms of trouble start to brew and the rains of disaster and hardship start to fall, and . . . The Bible says the house built on the sand falls every time and great is the fall! So much for homemade, homespun, personally created gods.

So, the one true God—the God who created us in His image (not vice-versa)—reaches out to us in a way that really fits, not necessarily the way we want or imagine. God reaches out to us with His Son! What was He thinking? This does not fit our plan. This does not fit our preconceived notions. This does not fit our image of how God should act. What was He thinking? Actually, He was thinking of us. He had us and our needs in mind. In love, He even put our needs first.

God reaches out to us with His Son. His Son who suffers and dies. His Son who sacrifices and ransoms. His Son who lays down His life that our lives might be picked up. God's reaching out to us reflects His true nature—love. God reached out to us in this way because He loves us. God gives His Son as a free gift, a sacrifice we could never earn, a ransom we could never pay. Love is the motivation, His love for us.

This is not a God who will allow us to do whatever we want, that would be unloving and against His true nature. More than that, it would be harmful for those whom He loves. We truly think this is what we want from God. We truly believe this kind of god would serve us better, but when the winds rise and the storm brews and the rain falls, so does this self-styled god. A true, loving God cannot stand by and watch those He loves self-destruct. He acts—He has to act. He acts in love. He sends His Son.

"I wish God would let me do whatever I want to do!" Be thankful we have a God who loves us too much to let this happen!

The Children (Not the Adults!) of God

For you did not receive a spirit that makes you a slave again to fear, but you received the Spirit of sonship. And by him we cry, "Abba, Father." The Spirit himself testifies with our spirit that we are God's children. Now if we are children, then we are heirs—heirs of God and co-heirs with Christ, if indeed we share in his sufferings in order that we may also share in his glory. (Rom. 8:15–17)

164

In His Presence

There is a story about a little boy who burst into the throne chambers of a medieval king. The boy was skipping and laughing and singing as children do. He was completely oblivious to the regal sobriety of his surroundings. Suddenly, he was intercepted by an armored soldier. "Have you no respect lad?" hissed the soldier. "Don't you know that the man on the throne is the king?"

The little boy wiggled out of the soldier's grasp and as he danced away he laughed and said, "He may be your king, but he is my father!" And the little boy bounced up the steps to the throne and jumped into the king's lap.

I remember coming to Peace Lutheran Church and School. I remember bringing my entire family to church for the first time. I remember a certain little girl named Mikal Soo who tried, unsuccessfully, to make her way up to where her father was leading worship. Every time she was intercepted by Sara, but not before the majority of the people noticed. Of course, the congregation thought it was cute. After all, she was not their child! Sara, on the other hand, took a slightly more serious view of the ordeal. Dad? Well, he was loving it, but, of course, he could not let his wife know!

Why did she want to be up front? What was the attraction? Most Lutherans seem to be excited about the back! It was not the "up front" she wanted. She wanted to be with her father. Perhaps she might have said, "He may be your pastor, but he is my father!"

How important is it for us to be in the presence of our Father? Not our earthly father, but rather, our perfect, loving, heavenly Father. Perhaps we feel distanced from our Father. Perhaps we struggle with guilt, and, as a result, avoid His presence. Perhaps, we do not understand the loving, fatherly relationship that is ours as a child of God. Perhaps we need to readjust our thinking about our God.

Our Father in heaven has such great love for us that He sent His only Son Jesus so we might be reunited with Him. Yes, we are sinful. Yes, we are guilty. Yes, we are separated from our Father by these corrupt and dark realities, but, but God sent His Son to bear our sins, to carry our guilt, to bridge the chasm caused by these corrupt realities. And Christ the Son carried this burden to a cross and paid the price and set us free from the burdens.

So, the reality for God's children is that we are God's children! He is our Father—our loving, our caring, our forgiving, our nurturing, our embracing Father. This reality changes us and changes our perspective. We no longer shrink from His glare with fear and terror. Now we embrace His presence with joy and delight!

It is with joy that we live in His presence. We cherish our relationship with Him through Christ. We do not fear His thoughts and feelings toward us because of the blood of Christ. He certainly remains our King, but He is also our Father!

Can you imagine running into the presence of your heavenly Father, jumping into His lap, and being encircled with His loving arms? Can you imagine that? He can!

For he has rescued us from the dominion of darkness and brought us into the kingdom of the Son he loves, (Col. 1:13)

CHAPTER SIXTEEN

Daddy, Fix It!

Children love to play with balloons. My children are no different. Balloons can change the attitude of the day! One balloon and the cloudy skies immediately clear. One balloon and sour turns sweet. Just one balloon—but, balloons are fragile. And, as you know, just as balloons do not last forever, neither do the moods they help create. The truth is, balloons worry me. My wife worries they will pop and scare the life out of her. I worry they will pop and deflate the sunny attitude they created!

One day, as the children returned from a birthday party, they came bearing balloons. Three balloons to begin with, but soon two, and not so long after, they were down to one. This is when Dad began to worry. So I did as dads do, I lined them up and warned them to be careful or they would soon be down to no balloons. Be careful how you hit it, be careful where you throw it, be careful how you treat it— please!

It is no secret as to what happened next. They messed around in all the wrong places, in all the wrong ways, they did all they were told not to do, and it popped! Along with the pop came the flooded eyes, the drippy noses, the pitiful whines. But this time it took a different direction. One of them grabbed the pieces of the balloon and led the processional to Dad. With the pieces held in little hands, the offering was stretched out to me, and they proclaimed, "Daddy, fix it!"

I am not helpless in repairing broken toys and such, but I can honestly tell you this was out of my field of experience.

In the beginning God created the heavens and the earth, and how beautiful and how perfect they were! Everything was in perfect working condition. Everything fit, everything functioned, everything was according to plan, everything was perfect. Into this beautiful and perfect place, God put man. They, too, were perfect, and what a delight they were to their Creator, and what a delight this wonderful, beautiful, perfect world must have been to them!

God told them they had free reign in this perfect place. He told them they were in charge of this beautiful creation. He told them they could do as they liked, enjoy all the wonders, eat the fruit, play with the animals, but—but do not eat of the fruit of that one tree. Just one tree. Do not eat the fruit. He told them that if they did they would destroy this beautiful world. The delightful place in which they lived would be ruined and would no longer delight them. In fact, it would become a difficult and miserable place. Sweat, tears, pain, sorrow, disasters, evil, darkness, and disease would fill the place once occupied by joy, peace, love, delight, happiness, health, and light.

Man did not listen. Man did not pay attention, at least not to God, and what He warned would happen, happened. The consequences of this sin became a reality. The perfect, earthly paradise was destroyed, and all that was left was a garden they could not enter. All that was left was misery, despair, and eventually death.

Man looked at what he had done. Man looked at the broken pieces and saw the brokenness all around him, and he looked up to his heavenly Father with tear-stained cheeks and repentant heart and said, "Daddy, fix it!"

And you know, He did! He sent His Son!

Direct me in the paths of your commands, for there I find delight. Turn my heart toward your statutes and not toward selfish gain. Turn my eyes away from worthless things; preserve my life according to your word. (Ps. 119:35–37)

CHAPTER SEVENTEEN

All that Glitters

Road tripping through northern California, cooped up in a too-small-for-five" vehicle in the middle of a seven-day rain ("it never rains in California"?), we came across a sign for a petrified forest. The children were four, five, and eight years, the journey was six hours, the parents were at wits end—it was time to stop. We pulled over to see some very hard, long-dead trees. The rain, however, would not stop, so we took shelter in the ever-present gift shop.

This particular gift shop specialized in rocks, a child's delight. Each child was allowed one purchase, within reason—my reason, since it would be my purchase. Mikal Soo decided to strike it rich. She discovered gold!

"Whoa! Check it out! Gold!"

I tried to explain, not gold—fool's gold—iron pyrite. She would have none of this. It looked like gold, it felt like gold, it was gold! After all, she was four years old and she knew gold when she saw it. Mikal Soo was not the first to be fooled by iron pyrite.

In the spring of 1608, the settlers at Jamestown, VA discovered gold. At least they thought it was gold. They almost completely abandoned their efforts at planting crops, preparing buildings, and making ready for winter, in order to devote themselves to the digging out and washing of this precious metal. The colonists probably would not have survived the winter had it not been for the Indians who fed them. However, they did manage to send back a shipload of this heavy metal. Unfortunately, their "gold" turned out to be fool's gold, iron pyrite. They had devoted all their time, their resources, their energies and talents to the pursuit of fool's gold!

All that glitters—From colonists, to four year olds, to every man, woman, and child of our world, we are constantly being fooled by things that glitter. Our world produces many paths that glitter with excitement. These paths promise glamour and fame and power and riches, and we are willing participants, willing travelers down these shining paths. Shining, but not real. Glittering, but not valuable. Sparkling, but only on the surface.

When we travel down such paths we complain of hollow and empty feelings. We struggle with depression and despair. We search for meaning. We ask, "Is this all there is?" Why? Because we have been fooled! The world has dangled its iron pyrite in front of us like a carrot, and we have gone chasing, wanting to believe that this is the answer, the path to true happiness and fulfillment. And, when we finally grab the carrot, when the goal is finally realized, when we have the desires of our heart in our hands, we discover the truth—we have been had! All that glitters . . .

The truth is this: There is no fulfillment as long as we remain separated from God. The truth is that as long as we may journey, as hard as we may work, as diligently as we may search, there is no way we will become one with God on our own. The truth is that we need help and not from man. The truth is that if we are to be reunited with God, and, thus truly find fulfillment, we are going to need God to clear the path back to Him. The truth is, this is what He did.

He sent His Son to clear the path. He sent His Son to pay the ransom for our sins and to open our lives to true riches. By the blood shed on the cross, we who were filthy dirty with sin have been shined and polished until we glow white, white as new snow! This is not the glamour and excitement promised, but undelivered, by the world—this is the fulfillment of truth and meaning for us, the creation of God.

Do not be fooled! Do not be led astray by the false-fronted allure of worldly riches. See the source of true riches, true meaning, true fulfillment in the Son. Because all that glitters is not gold!

Do not judge, and you will not be judged. Do not condemn, and you will not be condemned. Forgive, and you will be forgiven. Give, and it will be given to you. A good measure, pressed down, shaken together and running over, will be poured into your lap. For with the measure you use, it will be measured to you. (Luke 6:37, 38)

CHAPTER EIGHTEEN

Sitting on Your Blessings

It was time to escape. A time to abandon the phone, the meetings, the office and get away. Of course, it was only overnight! Christmas Day was past and the family and I drove to Oregon City to check out the end of the Oregon Trail and hide out in a hotel. Naturally, a visit to the Museum at the End of the Oregon Trail included the gift shop. The boys each got a souvenir that tied into the whole Oregon Trail theme. Mikal Soo got another stuffed animal. Same old story—The Hearst Castle, a stuffed seal—the Hausbarn in Manning, Iowa, a beanie baby—The End of the Oregon Trail, a stuffed fox. Nothing different, nothing unusual for Mikal Soo.

The next day arrived and it was time to make the journey north. We left the parking lot, got on the interstate, and off we went. That's when it started. "I can't find my fox! I forgot my fox! I left my fox at the hotel!" These were not calm statements of fact. These were statements delivered with a terrible, ear-piercing howl. Now, the same male, genetic make-up, which makes it impossible for me to feel comfortable in a mall and forbids me from asking directions, also makes it impossible for me to turn around. I cannot retrace my tracks—I just can't! And the howling continued.

My wife and I were on the edge, on the verge, close to . . . Twenty-five minutes later I managed to calm Mikal Soo down with some excellent child psychology—bribery—and we were able to finish our journey in relative peace. Back to Washington, back home to Bremerton. We drove up the driveway, got out of the van, and stretched our legs as Mikal Soo let out a whoop. "I found my fox! I was sitting on it!"

Oh, the ecstasy and the agony! Her ecstasy, our agony. She was sitting on the fox the whole entire time, the whole, entire trip, the whole entire wailing session. All she had to do—she did not even realize—it was right there!

Have you ever spent time with someone (an adult) who goes on and on about how terrible and unfair life is—his or her life? Have you ever sat there listening dumbfounded, because, as you did the mental checklist, it seemed that they had every reason to be ecstatic and no reason to be in agony? I have decided to call this malady the sitting-on-your-blessings syndrome. Guess whom I named it after?

The Lord God blesses us in so many ways. He pours out His blessings upon us day after day. He gives us pile after pile of things for which to give thanks. He constantly fills our cup to running over and we moan and groan. We wail and howl at the injustice of our lives, the unfairness of our circumstances, the green grass growing in our neighbor's yard. And, as we sit and howl, we do not seem to notice the bumps, the unevenness, the incongruities of what we are saying and where we are sitting. We are sitting on our blessings and have not yet noticed!

Blessing after blessing, pile after pile—how can we help but notice? Mikal Soo taught me that if you howl loud enough you can ignore or even miss reality. You can overlook your blessings! Sad because we are missing so much.

God's own Son, forgiveness, grace, joy, everlasting dwellings, comfort, peace. Freedom, food, clothing, shelter, transportation, freedom to worship, job, family. Friends, time, warmth, creation, community, service, opportunities, challenges. Blessing after blessing. Sitting on your blessings only accomplishes one thing—they stay warm and flat. They will not hatch and multiply. They will not go out and spread out. They will not fill your heart with joy as they fill the hearts of others.

These blessings are ours to use, and, in being used, they multiply. In being used they grow and spread. So, wipe your nose, dry your eyes, stand up, and take a look. Who knows what you will find! I promise you will find something— more than you think—more than you might imagine. Blessing after blessing to be used, and, in the using, to be enjoyed.

But seek first his kingdom and his righteousness, and all these things will be given to you as well. Therefore do not worry about tomorrow, for tomorrow will worry about itself. Each day has enough trouble of its own. (Matt. 6:33, 34)

CHAPTER NINETEEN

Seek Ye First

ook, Dad, there's an eagle nest over there—and there are some baby eagles in it!" "See that train way across the field? It has three engines and words on the side of the cars that say—" "Look at that lizard under the bush. It blends right in with the dead grass. See, it just moved!"

Amazing! These are the observations from the mouth of my son Jonathan. He notices everything. Nothing escapes his scrutiny. Nothing gets by his eye. Amazing! Amazing, because I spent half our vacation squinting, trying to see what he sees. Amazing, because Jonathan has only seven years of practice in the art of observation. Amazing, because my son, who can see a fish in the water under the moss from a moving car, cannot find his shoes! Every day it is the same ritual: "Where are my shoes?"

"Did you look under your bed?" "Where did you take them off yesterday?" "Try looking where you usually put them." "Jonathan, they are on your feet!"

Amazing! How can someone so observant, so alert, so tuned in to his surroundings not be able to locate his own shoes? It is a great mystery. In our house it is a great, unsolved mystery. As I visit with relatives and friends, I learn that this is a great, unsolved mystery in many houses.

This mystery goes beyond children. Consider the "seeing" abilities of adults. We are very tuned in to the physical, material surroundings of our world. We recognize the neighbor's new car. We observe beautiful, new houses going up. We scrutinize the news and learn of the "Microsoft millionaires" in our midst. As we do, we fail to see the shoes on our own feet. We miss the blessings that abound in our own lives. We overlook the more important, more personal abundance that has been piled upon us.

How can we miss this? Wrong eyes, wrong priorities, wrong goals. The Lord tells us to seek first the kingdom of God and all the rest will be added. Please note the order: The kingdom of God first! We turn things around. We seek first the things of our world, and, when we can work it into our schedule, we seek the kingdom. We shoot for the worldly riches, and, when we get old, we think of the kingdom. We focus in on the wealth available now and put off the untold riches promised by our King. Wrong priorities, wrong goals.

When we seek first the things of this world, it has an adverse effect upon our eyesight. Worldly eyes cannot see heavenly things. Worldly eyes fret and stew about the accumulation and overlook the treasure trove. Worldly eyes miss it! We miss the shoes on our feet, the blessings in our lives, the beautiful reality of God's kingdom.

God so loved that He turned His eyes toward us, not away. He so loved that He gave His only Son to pay the ransom that returned the greatest treasure to His children—

the treasure of eternal life. As God's children we have received the greatest of treasures, but God is not finished with His giving. His love and generosity have just begun. Each day, as we seek first His kingdom, as we seek to walk His path and follow His will, as we seek the things that are above and not the things below, God pours out more and more blessings. His blessings and abundance flow out to His people every day.

True, the people of God have trouble focusing. There is a lot of interference in this world. The distractions are many. Each day proves a new challenge for our fine tuning, focusing in abilities. Some days we see, really see it as it is; some days we cannot even see the shoes on our own feet! Each day is a challenge, but the blessings are there, and, properly focused, they are as plain as—the shoes on your feet!

Paul, a servant of God and an apostle of Jesus Christ for the faith of God's elect and the knowledge of the truth that leads to godliness—a faith and knowledge resting on the hope of eternal life, which God, who does not lie, promises before the beginning of time, and at his appointed season he brought his word to light through the preaching entrusted to me by the command of God our Savior. (Titus 1:1–3)

CHAPTER TWENTY

Promises, Promises

My wife says I talk too much about my children. She is probably right—she usually is right about such things—but I am always amazed at how accurately my children's behavior mirrors the behavior of the average child of God! As I have said before, this is undoubtedly why we are called the children of God and not the adults of God.

Well, that's my excuse for talking about my children all the time and I'm sticking to it!

As a pastor, I spend a lot of time coming and going. Coming home from this meeting, going to attend that meeting. Coming home from the care center, going to visit people in the hospital. Coming from here, going to there. In fact, there are days when I do not know if I am coming or going. Sometimes my children cannot figure it out, either.

On one such day a few years back, I picked up my little girl to hug and kiss her goodbye. I told her I had to go to church, but I would be right back. Mikal Soo looked into my eyes for a moment, then she reached down and took hold of my wrist and began to pull on my watch. At first I thought she wanted me to show her what time I would be back, but no! She pulled my watch off my wrist and said, "You can have it when you come back!"

At first I was hurt! She did not believe me! Had I ever told her I would be right back and not showed up as promised? Of course, it happens, but I mean lately, this week, maybe? OK! Sometimes I make promises that become impossible to keep, or that I forget about, or that I do not consider all that important, or . . . A promise is a promise.

How often are we like children when we hear the promises of God? We listen, we contemplate, and deep in our hearts, we would like to find a way to hold God hostage so He will be certain to remember and follow through? Even though God has never failed to keep a promise, we are so immersed in the unfaithfulness of our world we find it hard to trust. From theologians to politicians, from tax forms to school tests, we witness and even participate in dishonesty. The message? You cannot trust anyone. You cannot expect people to stand by their word. You cannot trust people to keep their promises. From this message it is only a short brain wave to God!

Thank goodness God does not operate with the standards of man. Thank goodness His value, moral, and ethical code is the top of the charts. Thank goodness! This is why God's promises are sure. Check out His track record: Promised to send His only Son to go to a cross to be the perfect sacrifice for the sins of all mankind so that we might be acceptable in His eyes once again—a promise kept! There is really no need to go any further, because if God loves us so much to keep a promise of this magnitude, we have no reason to believe He will not keep every other promise He has made. In fact, God's nature is such that He cannot break a promise. Wow! There are a few people in our world I would like to endow with the same nature! Of course, I also have three children who would like to endow me with the same nature!

Promises may be cheap in our society, our culture, our world, but for God, breaking a promise is not an option. That is a good thing. You can count on it. It is one of those promises made to us by God (see Titus 1:2)!

Conclusion

Well, there they are—*my kids*! All the warts and waves, all the blemishes and blushes, all the pimples and dimples—my kids. I think a lot of them in case this has not yet been made clear! I love them and am always amazed by them. Sometimes this amazement borders on despair, while at other times, it nears rapture. I suppose children are like that—I suppose your children are like that. Children, what a blessing!

As I have said before, I am somewhat confused as to why God would grant such a blessing. Why would He entrust into our care such a precious commodity? Why would He leave us in charge of fragile minds when we cannot even control our own thoughts and actions? Why give us children to raise and nurture in the ways of the Lord when we struggle with our own walk? Maybe His plan is to use these beautiful gifts to open our eyes. Open our eyes to His love, open our eyes to our responsibilities, open our eyes to His most important truths, open our eyes to our own "child-likeness." Maybe—something to ponder!

My children have certainly opened my eyes. They have broadened my understanding of our Lord and God and of His ways and His plan. They have made me a better theologian and a more practical preacher. And, of course, they have given me the opportunity to brag about my family from the pulpit, where decorum discourages leaving the room!

In the course of writing this book, my children have grown . . . and grown . . . and grown. Seven years is a long time in the development of a child. Many changes, and someday the world will no longer see them as children, but I always will. They are my children, regardless of age. My children, forever, just as we are God's children, forever!